HUNGARY

HUNGARY

Series editor:
Michael Shichor

Inbal Travel Information Ltd.
P.O.Box 39090 Tel Aviv Israel 61390

Intl. ISBN 965-288-069-8

Text: Menachem (Chemi) Shkolnik

Distributed in the United Kingdom by:
Kuperard (London) Ltd.
30 Cliff Rd.
London NW1 9AG

U.K. ISBN 1-870668-43-X

CONTENTS

TABLE OF MAPS

Preface

Although politically separated from western Europe for more than forty years, Hungary has always been unique among the states of the Eastern Bloc. Its people were the first to rise, unsuccessfuly, against the Communist regime (1956) and culturally always kept their orientation to the West.

No wonder then that Hungary was the first state in the Eastern Bloc to denounce Communism and embark on a "quiet revolution", in order to move from a rigid and conservative Communist system into a modern, free-market one. This revolution is still going on and a visitor to Hungary will see much evidence to this fact. But he is about to discover much more: the tastes of the traditional Hungarian cuisine, the typical sounds of its music, the impressive architecture of the beautiful city of Budapest and magical vilages where old pre-communist customs and traditions survived.

The changes mentioned above, made compiling this Guide a very complicated task. We added, erased and updated information almost till the last moment before the book went to print.

The staff of Inbal Travel Information made all efforts to produce the most updated and comprehensive Guide. It was headed by Chemi Shkolnik, an experienced and seasoned travaller who researched and spent time in Hungary gathering the information and the practical tips. We are sure that the effort invested in compiling this Guide will be justified by your enhanced enjoyment.

Michael Shichor

Using this Guide

In order to use this Guide in the most efficient way, we recommend that you read the following advice and act upon it.

The Guide includes a great deal of data meant to help you find your way and ensure that you see as much as possible with maximum saving of time, money and effort.

Before setting out, read the Introduction in its entirety. It provides the essential information you will need to know and understand before making the advance arrangements for your trip. Reviewing the material thoroughly, and acting upon it, means that you will be better organized and prepared for your visit.

The basic guideline in all of "MICHAEL'S GUIDE" publications is to survey places primarily in geographical sequence and not a thematic one. A geographical plan not only ensures the most efficient use of time, but also contributes dramatically to getting to know an area in its different aspects and acquiring a feel for it. Furthermore, you will be directed from a museum to a recommended restaurant or entertainment place, incorporating in your visit to one site several other locations which you may not have thought or heard of beforehand.

The chapters on main cities include maps and indexes of sites that will help you find out your way. On reaching each city, the Guide will direct you to recommended acommodation and restaurants. The maps will assist you in getting from one place to another.

There is a detailed index of all the places and sites covered in the Guide, at the end of the book.

The Hungarian language is probably unlike any language you are familiar with. It is far removed from Latin or any of its derivative tongues. For your convenience, therefore, we have added a short dictionary and a pronunciation key, at the end of the book. The useful words it contains may help you while travelling around the country.

At press time, information contained in this Guide was correct, but it is possible that you may discover certain inaccuracies due to unforeseen changes, and for that we apologise.

It is crucial that you check local information as much as

possible when you actually arrive in Hungary. A good source of information is your hotel reception or local tourist board information office. Most towns have an information office open during the summer season and details are given under the appropriate sections.

In order to keep ourselves updated, we are in need of your help. The cooperation of those who enjoyed what this Guide has to offer is essential, and ensures that those who follow you, will have as much accurate information at their disposal as you did. For this purpose we have included a short questionnaire at the end and would be grateful, if you were to answer in and return it to us.

Have a good and enjoyable trip!

INTRODUCTION

Part One — Getting to know Hungary

History of Hungary

From the pre-historic period until the Roman Conquest

Near the village of Vértesszőlős, between Budapest and Győr, ruins were discovered of a very ancient settlement, which evidently had existed there half a million years ago. In all of Europe, only the ruins found in Nuremberg, Germany, are older. The tribe which inhabited this ancient settlement left no other traces. However, the Neanderthals who hunted mammoths for subsistence, and other human species known to us today, have left considerable evidence of their existence, about 100,000 years ago, on pre-historic sites. A unique site which has been studied with great care can be found at Lovas, near Lake Balaton. The source of the red pigment used tens of thousands of years ago to resemble blood in ancient hunting and burial ceremonies was discovered there. Incidentally, pre-historic inhabitants did not exploit the shores of Lake Balaton because the place did not exist at that time. The age of the lake is estimated at only 20,000 years.

The neolithic period in Hungary, approximately 5,000-2,000 BC, is characterized by primitive agriculture, which Balkan immigrants apparently brought with them, along with the idea of domesticating local wild animals, especially cattle and pigs. Also, during that period there were large waves of immigration moving across the continent in search of food and fertile land. During the Bronze Age (2,000-800 BC) new ethnic groups armed with iron weapons made their appearance. They excelled in training horses and controlled vast areas of land. The most powerful groups, such as the Illyrians, the Thracians, and the Scythians, established an independent settlement, where a unique local culture developed.

The last wave of immigration which inundated most of Hungary, before the coming of the Romans, was made up of fighting Celtic tribes. They came from the east after having suffered defeat in Greece during the 3rd century BC. They brought with them new fighting techniques, as well as the arts of metallurgy and glass-blowing. The Celts built fortresses for defense and as a means of consolidating their control over regions they had conquered. Among these, was the stronghold of Ak-Ink, (meaning "abundant water") on Gellért Hill. The Romans used this name for their city Aquincum, located on the site of present-day Budapest.

From the Roman period until the coming of the Magyars

The attempts of the Emperor Augustus to create a barrier between the Romans and the barbarians in the east brought about the conquest of the Trans-Danube (the area west of the Danube) in the 1st century AD. Soldiers of the legions designated the part of the Danube which lies between Vienna and Budapest as the natural border between them and the barbarians to the east and to the north. They built army camps and fortifications along the river. The conquered area was set up as the province of Pannonia. It, in turn, was divided into two parts: Upper Pannonia (in what is now northern Transdanubia) and Lower Pannonia, whose capital, Aquincum, developed around a large army camp in an area which is part of the Hungarian capital of today.

Between the 1st and 4th centuries AD Pannonia flourished. Fortified cities rose around the army camps, containing impressive public buildings and elegant private homes in the best Roman tradition. The contact with culture from the west, which was introduced by the conquerors, bore fruit: trade routes were established, and Roman strongholds such as Scrabantia (Sopron), Sabaria (Szombathely), and Sopianae (Pecs) became administrative and commercial centers. These were the beginnings of the major cities in Hungary's history.

The disintegration of the mighty Roman Empire had its effect on the Hungarian provinces from the middle of the 3rd century AD onward. Nomadic tribes, Germanic and others, wrought havoc in the provinces, sowing death and destruction. The main force which emerged in Northeast Asia was the Hun tribes, who set out on a sweeping campaign to vanquish a disintegrating Rome. Led by Attila, they conquered Pannonia in the 5th century AD on their way to Rome, the heart of the western world at that time. The Huns were capable and cruel warriors with an excellent command of their weapons and horses. They subjugated the peoples whose land they had conquered and conscripted them into their army.

With Attila's death in 453 AD and the revolt of the Germanic tribes, the country was plunged into a turbulent period of warfare, which lasted for many years. After the Germanic tribes were banished by the Lombards, they in turn were forced out by the Avars, who came from Central Asia. The Avars brought with them two hundred years of relative quiet and stability, until the coming of the Magyars, the ancestors of the inhabitants of Hungary today.

The Magyars

The Magyar tribes which conquered Hungary at the end of the 9th century belong to the Finno-Ugric peoples. They lived in the Ural Mountains and steppes, where they developed a unique language and their own religion and culture. According to their tradition, as preserved in the Finnish saga, the Kalevala legends, the world was created from the egg of a wild duck which they considered holy.

After the western tribe broke up during the second milennium BC, it began to wander, eventually reaching Finland, while the Ugrics began moving toward the center of the continent. During these long years of wandering, the Ugric branch divided into extended tribes, including the Vogul, the Ostyak, and of course the Magyars, whose name means "talking people." The wandering tribes surrendered to the more powerful Huns. After the Huns were forced out of Hungary, the Magyars, starting in the 6th century, joined in an alliance of ten tribes located in the region of the Don River, led by the Huns and the Khazars, who had subjugated other peoples. The pact was called "Ten Arrows Covenant" (On-Ogur), and that is the source of the name Hungary.

In the 9th century, the Magyars cast off the Khazar yoke and began to move in the direction of the Carpathian Basin and the Danube. The tribes were led by three leaders, who divided the tasks of governing. Their status was equivalent to that of princes. Among them, Arpád stood out. He was apparently the military commander who led the conquest during the years 895-896 AD. The Magyar army completed the conquest with the help of local tribes, continuing to expand westward, mainly toward Italy and France. The fear which they inspired in those they conquered was expressed in a special supplement to the Christian prayer: "May God deliver us from the Hungarian arrows." Their belligerency continued until they were defeated by Emperor Otto I on the Lech Plain near Augsburg in 955.

After the failed attempts at expansion, descendants of Arpád (who died at the beginning of the 10th century after 40 years of rule) were free to consolidate their rule in Hungary. Arpád's grandson Taksony, who wanted the support and recognition of western Europe, asked the Pope to send a Bishop to Hungary in order to establish Christianity there. The Germans, fearing a Hungarian bishopric which would be directly responsible to the Holy See, prevented the Pope's representative from reaching his destination. During the days of Prince Géza, the great-grandson of Arpád, missonaries did indeed arrive, and Bruno of St. Glen was appointed Bishop of the Hungarians. Upon the death of his father (in 997), István, the son of Géza, ascended the throne, and with the support of the Pope, on Christmas Day of the year 1,000, he was crowned as the first Christian King of Hungary. The representative of the Pope, Bishop Gellert, helped the new king to spread Christianity in Hungary and to organize the tribes which were under his rule into administrative regions in the spirit of the times.

The kings of the House of Arpád who followed also tried to strengthen the government and the Church. Under the pressure of the aristocracy, descendants of leaders of the Magyar tribes, King Andrew II signed the "Golden Bull" — (the name comes from the golden seal which was affixed to the document) a bill of rights which enumerated the rights of the aristocracy and the bureaucracy. The Mongol invasion (1241) bathed the country in blood and destruction for an entire year until they moved on to continue their campaigns elsewhere. The efforts of King Béla IV to rebuild his country were successful despite his struggle with the aristocracy, who tried to exploit the weakness of the army and the state following the defeat in order to demand additional rights. The death of King Andrew III (1301) who left no heirs brought an end to the rule of the House of Arpád.

Various foreign kings and noblemen tried to seize control of the country, but the nobility crowned the Pope's candidate, Charles Robert from the Italian-French Anjou dynasty. His son Louis I died leaving no heirs (1382), and Sigismund of the House of Luxembourg succeeded him. He married Maria, daughter of Louis. The new king was despised by the Hungarian nobility for his exhibitionism and his conceit which earned him the nickname "Czech pig." After this hated king died, the nobleman János Hunyádi assumed power. He was appointed general commander in order to prepare for war against the advancing Turks. Hunyádi enjoyed the support of the people. When the Turkish threat dissipated following their defeat at Belgrade (1456), and the nearby Transylvanian princes began to show an interest in the Hungarian crown, a quick court revolt brought to the throne (1458) Hunyádi's son, Matthias Corvinus.

The reign of King Matthias and his wife, Queen Beatrix, is considered to be the Golden Age of medieval Hungary. The king worked to make peace among the nobility and to ease the tax burden of the peasants. He developed the legislative and judicial systems and established the "Black Army," which ensured the security of the state. His wife Beatrix, a lover of the arts, supported a cultural renaissance which included development of the sciences, encouragement of artists, and the construction of royal palaces in Buda and in Visegrad. The kings who succeeded Matthias upon his death (1490) were less successful than he, and there was much corruption in the country and in the royal court. Against this background, several local revolts broke out which were suppressed very brutally by the kings who were controlled by the nobility (for example King Louis II was crowned when he was only nine years old). This deterioration continued until the battle of Mohács in 1526.

Foreign conquest — From the battle of Mohács until the War of Independence

After they captured Belgrade in 1521, the Ottoman forces mounted a new campaign against the Hungarians in an effort to expand the influence of Islam and of the Sultanate. Facing King Louis II and his 25,000 soldiers were about 100,000 Turkish fighters under the command of the most famous Ottoman Sultan, Suleiman the Great.

The Battle of Mohács, which lasted for several hours on August 29, 1526, was a clearcut defeat for the Hungarian army: the king, many of his officers, and half of his soldiers were killed. The country lost its independence for the next three hundred years.

After the Turks conquered Buda in 1541, Hungary was in fact divided into two. The Austrian House of Hapsburg held the region now known as "North Transdanubia" as a barrier between Vienna and the Turkish conquerors who controlled central Hungary. Local aristocrats ruled Transylvania with the approval of the Turks. The Moslem Turkish regime imposed heavy taxes on the local population in order to finance its military escapades, but it did not interfere in religious matters which were the subject of continual internal strife between Protestants and Catholics.

The weakening of the Ottoman Empire in the 17th century, both internally and internationally, was exploited by the Austrians to repulse the Turkish threat to Vienna and to mobilize an international force. In the difficult battles which took place during the 1680's, this force managed to expel the Turks from Hungary, after 150 years of Ottoman occupation. In 1686 Buda was conquered, and a few years later, the Hungarians discovered that although they had been liberated from one foreign occupier, they had fallen into the hands of another — the House of Hapsburg — which had every intention of ruling over them and treating their country as a peripheral appendage of Austria. The ferment among the Hungarians broke out in a revolt under the leadership of Ferenc Rákóczi. Rákóczi, the son of rich Transylvanian nobility, called for revolt against the Hapsburgs (1703) and led his war with much popular support for eight years. He was eventually defeated by the superior might of his opponents and exiled to Turkey, where he died alone. The Hapsburg rulers tightened their grip on Hungary, they encouraged various minority groups to immigrate to Hungary, and they destroyed palaces and fortresses which had been used in the revolt. Thus, they added ruin to the destruction that had already been caused in the wars against the Turks.

At the beginning of the 19th century, Hungary enjoyed a period of tranquility. The Empress Maria Theresa had instituted many reforms starting in the middle of the previous century which gave the country economic and national momentum. Her flagbearers were Count István Széchenyi and the brilliant publicist and orator Lajos Kossuth. Széchenyi was responsible for vigorous economic development and for an impressive wave of construction in the Baroque style. Kossuth promoted an awareness of national uniqueness and cultural heritage among Hungarians.

From the War of Independence until the end of the Second World War

In Pest on March 15,1848, an uprising broke out, led by the poet Sandor Petőfi. It quickly developed into a full-scale war of independence aimed at breaking away from the House of Hapsburg. At Debrecen in April 1849 this separation was indeed proclaimed. The Austrian Emperor Francis Joseph I turned to the Russian Czar for help, and together, they put down the Hungarians in August 1849. Although the military campaign ended in defeat, the Hungarian War of Independence made the Austrians aware of the strength and rights of their eastern neighbors. In 1867, this recognition brought about the famous compromise of Ausgleich according to which one king would rule over the two sovereign peoples as the basis of the Austro-Hungarian Empire. Although that one king was the Hapsburg Emperor Francis Joseph, still the Hungarians gained their own government, with the right to determine internal policies.

This "period of dualism" continued until the First World War and was a time of tremendous growth and progress in all areas of life. Industries were established, the standard of living rose, the arts flourished, and architectural masterpieces were built (such as the royal palace in Budapest which was renovated and rebuilt in the Baroque style).

The First World War brought the collapse of the Austro-Hungarian alliance with the fall of the House of Hapsburg. On November 16, 1918 Hungary was declared an independent republic. Turmoil in the young republic caused frequent changes of government between the Social Democrats headed by Mihály Károlyi and the Communists led by the Jewish ideologist Béla Kun. The Communists tried to impose their will on the people, with the help of special police units, quickly labelled the "Red Terror." In opposition, the army and the aristocracy used the "White Terror" to strike at the Communists. In 1920 the Hungarian National Council, fearing internal strife and civil war, made the mistake of choosing as ruler a strong man, Admiral Miklós Horthy, who called for a return to the old order and to former national values.

After the defeat it suffered in World War I and tired of its internal conflicts, Hungary signed the Treaty of Trianon (1920) in which it lost two thirds of its territory and over half its population to its neighbors. Most painful of all was the loss of Transylvania with its 1,500,000 Hungarians to Romania, causing bitterness and tension between Hungary and Romania to this very day.

The government of Horthy made Hungary into an inflexible nationalist republic, where, gradually, peasants, workers, and various minority groups, first among them the Jews, lost their rights. The Nazis, who came to power in Germany, found the Hungarian ruler to be a willing ally, and he remained in power almost until the end of World War II.

At the beginning of World War II Hungary maintained a pseudo-neutrality, while actually supporting the Nazis and eventually joining the Axis powers (1941). Still, life remained relatively peaceful until March 1944 when the Nazis occupied Hungary after Horthy had declared its neutrality in anticipation of a Russian invasion. The Arrow-Cross Party came to power and sent bands of Fascist ruffians into the streets. Among their victims were Jews and others, murdered in the streets and thrown into the Danube.

The Russian blockade of Budapest, accompanied by numerous bombardments, lasted for the entire winter of 1945. By February 13 when the city was conquered by the Red Army, three quarters of its buildings had been destroyed or badly damaged. By April 4 all of Hungary had been liberated.

The Communist period

In the elections of November 1945 the Center Party won, but the

Soviets forced it to include Social Democrats and Communists in the government. After a short period, the Communists gained control and, in 1948, Hungary was declared a one-party republic. That one party was the Communist Workers Party, of course, led by Mátyás Rákosi, Stalin's loyal ally in Hungary. The new regime relied upon the Avo, the notorious secret police.

Stalin's death in 1953 brought a change of government in Hungary. The uncompromising Rakosi was replaced by the more flexible Imre Nagy. The Hungarian intelligentsia, which had never been happy with the Communist regime, felt a sense of liberation and began to agitate for reform. Tension reached its peak in October 1956 when students demanded democratization of the state. Afraid of the unrest, the government tried to clamp down once again, but it was too late. On November 1 Hungary announced its withdrawal from the Warsaw Pact and asked for United Nations backing. On the morning of November 4 the Russian invasion began. Within a few days, the Hungarian opposition was easily crushed and the regime began the mass arrest of its opponents. Two hundred thousand fled to the west. The west (particularly the United States), preoccupied with the Suez crisis, limited itself to verbal condemnation of the Russian actions.

The Russians appointed János Kádár to lead the nation and the party. Special government courts were set up aimed at combating any manifestation of opposition or unrest; the death sentence was imposed as was exile to the Soviet Union.

János Kádár initiated the policy of five-year plans to rehabilitate Hungary. The result was that after thirty years, Hungary was on the verge of bankruptcy. Kádár was forced to institute various reforms, but they were not very successful, and he was pushed aside along with his outdated administrative and economic methods.

The turnabout

Today, Hungary is in the midst of a revolution: changes are taking place rapidly. An economic breakthrough actually occurred at the end of Kádár's government, with private enterprise being allowed in various spheres, but it seemed that the reforms were too slow and too few. The revolution began at the party conference in May 1988 at which Kádár and other politburo members who had supported the conservative policies were forced out of office. Károly Grosz was elected to head the party. To head the government he appointed a young economist, a Harvard graduate, who initiated a number of daring political and economic policies in an attempt to save Hungary from imminent bankruptcy. This turnabout was accompanied by democratization — new parties were established, the right to freedom of expression was expanded, and daring business initiatives were undertaken in order to free the economy from its traditional centralization.

Hungarians are divided in their opinions about these innovations and are a little confused by the speed of the changes. There is fear of unrest due to economic shortages, spiraling inflation, the appearance of a class of nouveaux riche, and the weakening position of the poor classes. The process is only beginning. Free elections were held in early 1990 and in May, a coalition government was formed.

Landmarks in Hungarian history

1st century BC-4th century AD — the Romans establish the province of Pannonia.

430 — Invasion of the Huns.

896 — Magyar conquest.

1000 — Crowning of King István I and beginning of the spread of Christianity in the country.

1241 — Invasion of Mongol tribes and destruction of most of the cities in the country.

1458-1490 — Government of King Matthias. The independent Hungarian kingdom is at its height.

1526 — Defeat by the Ottoman Army at the battle of Mohács. Disintegration of the regime and beginning of the Turkish occupation.

1541 — Conquest of Buda by the Ottoman army.

1683-1699 — Turks are driven out by the House of Hapsburg which regards Hungary as one of its provinces.

1703 — Revolt against the Hapsburgs, led by Ferenc Rákóczi.

1711 — Suppression of the Hungarian revolt by the Austrians and their allies.

1848 — Hungarian War of Independence and declaration of Hungarian independence in Debrecen.

1849 — Suppression of the Hungarian revolt.

1867 — Compromise agreement stating that Austria and

Hungary are equal nations having one king from the House of Hapsburg, but, two governments.

1918-1919 — Collapse of the House of Hapsburg after the First World War.

1920 — Hungary loses two thirds of its territory and its population to neighboring countries in the Treaty of Trianon.

1920-1944 — Hungary governed by Admiral Horthy who supports the Nazis.

1944 (March) — The Nazis take control of Hungary.

1945 (April) — The Soviet Army liberates Hungary from the Nazi yoke.

1956 (November) — Invasion by the Soviet Army to suppress the democratic awakening in Hungary. Kádár is appointed to lead the country.

1988 (May) — Kádár is deposed and a new government is set up which institutes very wide-ranging social and economic reforms in an attempt to combine Hungarian socialism with international economics and politics.

1990 — Democratic elections.

Geography

Hungary lies in the Carpathian Basin in Central Europe, between Austria (west), Yugoslavia (south), Romania (east), the Soviet Union (northeast), and Czechoslovakia (north). Today the country extends over an area of 93,032 kms. which is less than 1% of the entire continental land mass.

While the Carpathian Basin is surrounded by the Alps mountain range in the west, the Dinaric Alps in the south, and the Carpathians in the east, Hungary is mostly quite flat. The highest mountain in the country, Mount Kékesteto, east of Budapest, is only 1,015 meters high. Near Szeged is the lowest spot in the country, 78 meters above sea level.

The Danube River (Duna in Hungarian) is the second largest river on the continent (after the Volga), and it cuts across the country from north to south for 417 kms. The western part of the country is referred to as Transdanubia, and the eastern is divided between the Great Plain (Alföld) and the northern mountains. Between the Czechoslovakian border and Budapest, northwest of the capital, the river twists around and creates the Danube Bend (Duna-Kanyar) — one of the country's most beautiful regions. The River Tizsa flows for almost 600 kilometers through the country from the Russian border in the northeast to the Yugoslavian border in the south, fertilizing the Great Plain.

Lake Balaton, the largest lake in Central and Western Europe, covers an area of 600 sq. kms. in central Transdanubia and serves as a bustling vacation center. Throughout the country there are smaller rivers and lakes which supply an abundance of water for agriculture and industry, as well as for home use.

Approximately one sixth of the country's area is covered by forests, especially oak and beech trees. Five percent of the country's area has been proclaimed Nature Reserves in which plants and animals are protected by law.

Hungary's climate is temperate continental. January is the coldest month of the year, even though the average temperature for the month sometimes does not go below freezing. There is not much rain and snow in the country, but summer rains are possible even in the warmest months of July and August.

Economy

Hungary enjoys both an abundance of land suitable for agriculture and numerous possibilities for the industrial development of mines and quarries. Tourism is flourishing: during 1988, nineteen million tourists came to Hungary (only ten million people live in Hungary!). These facts indicate that the country, which is today on the brink of bankruptcy, possesses extensive economic potential.

Hungary's external debt is very large, and it was the shaky economic situation which forced János Kádár to resign. Hungarian economists and ordinary citizens alike accuse the Communist system and especially the Soviet Union of being responsible for this crisis. The Communist system brought nationalization, centralization, government bureaucracy, and five-year plans instead of a free market economy, and it eroded the motivation of workers and managers. The Soviet Union relocated to its own territory thriving industries which had been nationalized after the 1956 revolt and appropriated large development loans that had been allocated to Hungary and which Hungary must now pay back. The new Hungarian regime is attempting to break out of the economic bind by cutting budgets, encouraging private initiative and outside investment, raising prices, and imposing additional taxes, such as a highway toll.

In contrast to the scarcity in neighboring Romania, Poland, Czechoslovakia, and the Soviet Union, there is no shortage of food and clothing in Hungary. While the average monthly wage is low (about $120), many people work at a second and even a third job. Poverty is not in evidence in the markets, the shops, and the roads which bustle with vehicles from both Western and Eastern Europe making. However, it is difficult to acquire foreign currency for a trip abroad, and the price of a city apartment in a desirable neighborhood is equal to the amount a worker takes home during his entire lifetime. So far, it would seem that most of the public tend to go along with the economic direction which the government has taken. The government enjoys this support despite the decline in the standard of living and the unemployment which the economic leaders now openly acknowledge exists, for the first time in the Eastern bloc. All agree that government policy must lead to an improvement in the standard of living within the next few years and that plans and declarations alone are not enough.

Population

The origin of the Hungarian people is rooted in the Finno-Ugric nomads who lived in the Ural Steppes thousands of years ago. From the Urals, the Magyars advanced westward, reaching Hungary during the 9th century AD. The indigenous population was assimilated by the conquerors, and the Magyar people with its unique language and culture now constitutes about 97% of the total population. The largest minorities in the country include Germans (1.6%), Slovaks (1.1%), and Romanians. They were encouraged to emigrate as part of the policy of the House of Hapsburg during the 17th and 18th centuries. Approximately two million Hungarians live under Romanian rule in the region of Transylvania, which Hungary lost after the First World War as a result of the Trianon Treaty (1920). The attempt of the Romanian regime to assimilate the large Hungarian minority is a cause of tension between Hungary and Romania.

Today, there are 10,600,000 people in Hungary. Over two million people live in Budapest alone — more than in the ten next largest cities put together. Despite the Communist regime, Christianity retains a strong attraction for Hungarians. An overwhelming majority of the people are Catholics, and a minority are Protestants.

The Gypsies in Hungary

Although official censuses have not been carried out (apparently intentionally), the number of Gypsies in Hungary is estimated at between a quarter and a half million. They are descendants of lower caste Indian tribes who fled to Europe during the 12th century, preferring a marginal existence to establishing a well-ordered society. They are to be found today in almost every Hungarian city, working at jobs on the fringes of society: flower vendors, street cleaners, pickpockets, pimps, etc. There are permanent Gypsy enclaves in the poor neighborhoods outside the large and medium-sized cities and in the small villages in the northeastern part of the country. The Hungarians look down on the Gypsies, whom they refer to in Hungarian as *cigány* — an appellation of derision. The Gypsies, on the other hand, refer to themselves as *rom*. For their part, the Gypsies have little love for the Hungarians. The only "duet" the two peoples play together takes place in restaurants in which "Gypsy music" (*cigányzene*) is played by Gypsy orchestras who have taken Romanian, Balkan, and Magyar folksongs and imparted to them their own unique touch in the ancient emotional style. The Gypsies, most of whom live in poverty, do not appreciate visits of uninvited tourists in their settlements which are far from being tourist attractions. Hungarians themselves do not visit these places, and foreign visitors are also advised to refrain from such visits. "Gypsy Evenings" organized for tourists by travel agents are specially staged and are not authentic Gypsy celebrations.

The language

The tourist finds the Hungarian language strange and foreign-sounding. The difficulty goes far beyond learning several simple phrases which would enable the tourist to explain himself — it lies in the pronunciation of the words themselves. The polite Hungarians smile at the sound of the impossible accents coming from the lips of visitors. Many of the older generation speak German, a remnant of the Austro-Hungarian union, while the young people try to express themselves in English, largely without much success.

The unique Hungarian language is one of the Finno-Ugric languages. Influenced by Turkish, German, and Russian, it has departed greatly from Finnish, the language closest to it. In the linguistic appendix at the end of the book, we have presented several key words along with the correct pronunciation of the letters, but it would be preferable to show the written word to your Hungarian companion.

Culture and art

Culture and art are held in great esteem in Hungarian society and occupy a prominent place in daily life. With the artistic flowering which began during the 18th century, many artists have emerged who have greatly influenced Hungarian society. Literature, drama, and poetry are not accessible to the visiting tourist because of the limitations of language, but it should be noted that poets such as Sándor Petofi and playwrights like József Katona have achieved outstanding artistic accomplishments and are still much admired in Hungary.

The visitor to Hungary cannot help but be impressed with the place music has in the social life of the country. Concerts, operas, operettas, and musicals on the highest level are performed nightly on Hungarian stages. Important Hungarian composers include Béla Bartók and Zoltan Kodály and, of course, Franz Liszt, whose Hungarian Rhapsodies are well known to music lovers far beyond the boundaries of the country.

The concerts take place for the most part in elegant concert halls. They may be performed by such orchestras as the railway orchestra or the postal orchestra, which is not to imply that the violinists lick stamps or punch railroad tickets before concerts; rather, the orchestra is professional, and the musicians' salaries are paid by the treasury of the institution, according to regular Communist practice. In dance as well, the Hungarians have achieved much success. The dance troupe of Gyór, for example, has won international acclaim.

Outstanding painters include Munkacsi and Csontvary, whose work still influences artistic trends in the country. The artist Vasarely, who has played a central role in contemporary art, was born and raised in Pécs but lived for many years in France, so that the Hungarians refer to him only hesitatingly as a "Hungarian artist."

An additional art medium which developed in Hungary is ceramic sculpture which reached its apex in the marvelous works of the artist Margit Kovács. Exhibitions of her work have taken place in many cities and especially in Szentendre, located at the bend of the Danube, where she lived and worked for many years. Kovács' students established a new school and place Hungary in the front ranks in the world in this field.

Architecture

One of the things which makes a trip to Hungary so enjoyable is the beautiful buildings which have been constructed during the past thousand years. The contrast between city centers which were built in different styles before the Second World War and the prosaic housing developments which surround them, lacking any aesthetic sensitivity, is apparent in almost any urban center. In the centers of old cities a tourist can visit a living architectural monument to other times that no longer exist.

The Romanesque style: After the Dark Ages in Europe, which lasted from the fall of the Roman Empire until the 10th century, the continent began to stabilize and rebuild. The architect was in need of a new method of construction for housing and churches. The Romanesque style used the knowledge which remained from the Byzantine period, but did not keep the fixed and inflexible relationship between all the elements in the structure. Pointed roofs were built to prevent accumulation of too much snow on the high church tower, and the proliferation of towers, domes, gates, and chapels were intended to glorify the name of God and of Jesus, the saints and the ruler, by creating a number of centers. Most of the structures were built with thick stone walls and served as fortified shelters in time of need.

The Gothic style: This style originated and developed in France during the Middle Ages and quickly spread throughout Europe. In contrast to the solid massive Romanesque style structures, the Gothic style provided buildings which expressed magnificence and grandeur. An attempt was made to be free of the massiveness of the building by emphasizing vertical lines. The walls, relieved of the necessity of serving as massive supporting walls became large sunlit, embellished windows, adding to the feeling of airiness. The cathedrals, adorned with impressive stone engravings and pointed arches, added to the feeling of spaciousness without dwarfing the figure of the person who entered. The name Gothic had derogatory connotations during the Renaissance, being the name of one of the Teutonic tribes which destroyed Europe at the beginning of the Middle Ages. Renaissance people tended to regard this style as an expression of barbaric culture. Today, however, their negative evaluation seems mistaken in view of the impressive architectural achievements in this style. The Church of Matthew the Holy in Budapest is a good example of this style, and also the House of Parliament in the capital, built only in the 19th century, in a neo-Gothic style, using Gothic lines.

The Baroque style: The most prominent style in Hungary is the Baroque style. It flourished during the 17th and 18th centuries along with the building and renewal taking place in Hungary after the Turks were forced out. Many regard the Baroque as the highest level of development of the Gothic style, despite the fact that "Baroque" is a derogatory name meaning "fake jewel" used by 18th century lovers of Classicism. The Baroque style, which originated in the city of Rome, is characterized by the creation of dark empty spaces, lit by the carefully planned capture of the sun's rays passing through the colored windows. The lighting creates an atmosphere of holiness and mystery appropriate to the Catholic Church (which adopted this style officially). Other attributes of Baroque are the blurring of the borders between architecture, sculpture and painting, heightened dramatization, expression of intense feeling, rounded movements, and the use of elliptical and curving forms. The style was brought to Hungary by the House of Hapsburg which had made Austria an important Baroque center. The Baroque buildings give many cities their special character.

Hungarian names and leaders

The uniqueness of the Hungarian language is reflected in the common first names. Some of these names retain the heritage of the Magyar conquest. Arpád, for example, was the tribal leader, and Gyula was the title of the military commander of the tribe. Other names are distortions or are adapted from western sources, so that Michael becomes Mihály, Stephen is István, Margaritta is Margit, and Elizabeth becomes Erzsébet.

The leaders and intellectuals of Hungarian history are remembered with honor: almost every city has its Szécheny Street, Jókai Mór Square, etc. Here is a short sketch of some of the more well-known personages and key figures of the Hungarian heritage:

Arany János (1817-1882) — Well-known poet, composer, and literary translator.

Bajcsy-Zsilinsky Endre (1888-1944) — Leader of the anti-Fascist movement in the Second World War. Put to death by Arrow Cross Party.

Bartók Béla (1881-1945) — Famous composer of modern classical music much of which is based on Hungarian folk melodies.

Csontváry Kosztka Tivadar (1853-1919) — Much admired painter whose colorful works even today influence Hungarian painting.

Dobó István (? -1572) — Commander of Agar Fortress who prevented its conquest by the Turks.

Dósza Gyorgy (1474-1514) — Leader of the peasant revolt in 1514.

Erkel Ferenc (1810-1893) — Pianist, composer, and founder of the National Opera.

Hess András — One of the founders of printing in Hungary (15th century).

Hunyadi János (1407-1456) — Led Hungarian army in battle against the Turks; father of King Matthias.

István I (975-1038) — First Hungarian king, crowned on Christmas Day 1,000 A.D.

INTRODUCTION

Janus Pannonius (1432-1472) — Important bishop, also renowned as a poet.

Jókai Mór (1825-1904) — Very popular romantic writer.

József Attila (1905-1937) — Modern poet who committed suicide at a young age.

Katona József (1791-1830) — Playwright who shaped the Hungarian theater.

Kodály Zoltán (1882-1967) — Composer and music researcher who developed innovative methods of music instruction.

Kossuth Lajos (1802-1894) — Outstanding orator and statesman who led the revolt in Hungary in 1848.

Kun Béla (1886-1939) — Leader of the Workers' Party who led the country after the fall of the House of Hapsburg.

Liszt Ferenc (1811-1886) — Famous composer, founder of the music academy in Budapest.

Mátyás Corvin (1440-1490) — King of Hungary; during his reign, independent Hungary was at the height of its powers.

Móricz Zsigmond (1879-1942) — Well-known writer whose works have been translated into many languages.

Munkácsy Mihály (1844-1900) — Realistic painter, one of the outstanding 19th century Hungarian artists.

Petofi Sándor (1823-1849) — Poet and revolutionary; one of the leaders of the 1848 revolt.

Rákóczi Ferenc (1676-1735) — Hungarian prince from Transylvania, led the revolt in 1703.

Semmelweis Ignác (1818-1865) — Jewish doctor who discovered the connection between infection and the death of women in childbirth.

Széchenyi István (1791-1860) — An advocate of reform and a great innovator in the 19th century.

Táncsics Mihály (1799-1884) — Democratic, humanistic politician and writer.

Tóth Arpád (1886-1928) — Poet and literary translator.

Vorosmarty Mihály (1800-1855) — Beloved dramatic poet.

Ybl Miklós (1814-1891) — Architect who contributed much to construction of religious buildings.

Part Two — Setting out

Who's going?

The growing number of tourists coming to the country shows that a trip to Hungary is right for almost everyone. The concentration of historical sites and the wealth of musical and cultural offerings mean that a visit in Hungary will center more on a trip to the large cities than to natural and scenic sites, and that it is more appropriate for urban culture buffs than for back-packers looking for remote trails.

One can join organized trips, anything from guided tours lasting several hours in Budapest and costing $10 to trips lasting for several days. The country is not large, so it is possible to choose an interesting site, see it during a daytime trip, and return in the evening to Budapest. Such guided tours are offered in English and in German and reservations may be made through tourist agencies. Note that the *IBUSZ* bureau is the largest tourist bureau in the country and organizes many such tours. At the time you make your reservation, you should specify which language you would like the guide to speak.

Tourism is directed toward couples, and many of the sleeping accommodations in hotels, as well as in private homes, do not include rooms or prices for individuals but only for couples. This should not be a problem for women travelling on their own, since Hungarian graciousness and courtesy are of the highest level, and women travelling alone are not bothered.

During the summer season the shores of Lake Balaton are crowded with tourists, mostly German-speaking, who come to soak up the sun and to bathe in the lake. Those wishing to relax for several days during their trip may want to visit the lake whose shores are teeming with visitors throughout the tourist season. Another type of tourism popular in Hungary is health tourism at the thermal spas, which are rich in minerals that are beneficial for the body. Many tourists come expressly for dental treatment. Special appendices have been prepared for these tourists at the end of the book.

How to get there

All flights to Hungary arrive at the Ferihegy Airport near Budapest, where it is possible to get a Hungarian entry visa. Another possibility is to fly to Vienna or to Zagreb and from there to come by train to Hungary.

By train: Several international trains reach Hungary daily from neighboring countries. Train travel, especially in first class, is very pleasant, and the traveller arrives directly at the city centers. Trains arrive from Vienna (a 4-hours trip), Paris (21 hours), Munich (11 hours), Zurich (16 hours). The Mastral train, originating in Rome (21 hours), arrives via Zagreb (7 hours). The Romanian train from Bucharest is not at all recommended, since it makes many stops and has frequent inspections en-route.

Reductions on trains are given to young people and pensioners and on return tickets, etc. For **Eurail-pass** holders, the trip to Hungary is included in the price of the ticket. Railroad passengers must obtain their entry visa in advance and cannot enter at the border crossing.

By bus: This is the hardest way to reach Hungary and is recommended only for young people and back-packers. The trip from London lasts 50 hours and is very tiring. Buses also come from Yugoslavia and from Greece, but because of the length and nature of the journey, it is preferable to come by train and use the bus only for short trips inside the country.

By boat: One of the ways to reach Budapest is by sailing down the Danube River in a ferry from Vienna. During the trip, which lasts 4.5 hours, passengers can enjoy the scenery of the Danube Bend, as well as the convenient services on board. Ferry passengers arrive at the dock in the center of the city. They will need to arrange visas in advance: visas will not be issued to those entering the country via the river.

By car: This is a recommended way of travelling inside Hungary or in the neighboring countries. People who rent cars outside the country will arrive in Hungary via one of the excellent international highways, such as E5 from the west (Austria) and E96 from the south (Yugoslavia) or via one of the many border crossings, open 24 hours a day, on the internal roads connecting Hungary with its neighbors. Visitors arriving by car can get visas at the border.

When to come

The official tourist season begins on May 1 and ends at the end of October. These months are the recommended time for your visit weatherwise, although the period between the middle of June and the end of August is the height of the tourist season, when visitors fill the hotels, restaurants, shops, and vacation spots near Lake Balaton.

The ideal time for a trip is from May until mid-June, and from September until mid-October. Those coming in April risk changeable but not unbearable weather. The weather does not vary drastically and is more or less the same throughout the country.

Holidays and events

Holidays in Hungary are either anniversaries of important dates in Hungarian history (for example, the date of liberation from the Nazis) or else religious holidays (such as Christmas and Easter). On these holidays all government and private institutions are closed except for emergency services, transportation, and basic tourist services.

January 1 — New Years Day
April 4 — Day of liberation from the Nazis
April — Easter (the exact date varies)
May 1 — May Day (workers' holiday)
August 20 — Constitution Day
October 21-23 — Republic Day
December 25-26 — Christmas

The following is a local calendar of events, which take place in different cities and villages throughout Hungary (for additional information, contact local tourist agencies, also see heading "Special Events" which has a separate section for each city):

March — Busó Mask Carnival at Mohács near Pécs. Annual spring festival in Budapest and in Sopron (featuring dance, music, and drama).

"Spring Days" of Szentendre (historical dramas).

May — Annual trade fair in Budapest.

Alba Regia Days in Székesfehérvár (including concerts in the old style using ancient instruments).

June — Village fair in Orség (arts and crafts exhibition and an open market).

July — Folklore festival in Kalocsa and Kecskemét (folk entertainment, dancing, and costumes)

Historical festival in Esztergom (music using ancient instruments).

Jazz festival at Debrecen.

Anna Báll Festival in Balatonfüred (beauty queen selected).

Theater festival in Gyula (theater in an ancient fortress).

August — Carnival of flowers in Debrecen and village fair in Hortob gy (August 20).

Pottery festival in Veszprém (pottery exhibit and sale).

Auto racing "The Big Prize."

Theater festival in Kőszeg (theater in an ancient fortress).

Wine harvest celebration in Boglárlelle near Lake Balaton (popular celebration focusing on wine).

September — Wine harvest at Badacsony on the shore of Lake Balaton.

Fine arts festival in Budapest — exhibitions and special events at museums and galleries, concerts, and plays.

International trade fair in Budapest.

How long to stay

Hungary is not a large country. The trip should focus on beautiful Budapest with its wealth of tourist attractions. You will want to devote several days to this interesting city. Don't miss spending at least one day in the area around the Danube Bend, just north of Budapest.

A trip to the region of Transdanubia and Lake Balaton will take about 3-5 days (depending on the number of days you want to spend vacationing at the lake), and 3-5 additional days are needed in order to visit the Great Plain and mountains in the north.

How much does it cost?

Hungary is an inexpensive and well developed country for tourists despite its inflation and economic difficulties. Hotel rooms, when available, are not expensive; and public transportation, entertainment, public baths and, of course, restaurants are very cheap. Often tourists are amazed at the reasonable prices.

Average prices (in American dollars):

Hotels
5 stars — $70-$140 (found only in Budapest).
4 stars — $80-$100.
2-3 stars — $40-$60.
1-star, pension — $15-$25.
Room in private home — $6-$18 (without breakfast).
Youth (or other) hostel — $3-$5 for a bed in a room with several other people.
Camping — $4-$6 to use the grounds and $1 extra to use the conveniences (water, electricity, etc.)

Restaurants (full meal for a couple, including wine)
Very expensive restaurant — $40-$50.
Expensive restaurant — $25-$40.
Medium-priced restaurant — $15-$22.

Inexpensive restaurant — $5-$15.

The law requires every restaurant to offer its customers a fixed price inexpensive menu (Menű) of two or three courses at a price of about $2 (for the benefit of the workers). The young and the young at heart enjoy ordering these filling meals, even though restaurant owners tend to claim that they are out of the daily special, which indeed is the case after the early noon hours.

Transportation
Interurban train and bus fares are very low, despite recent increases, and amount to only a few dollars for each trip. Bus and subway fares are incredibly cheap by western standards (a ride on the Budapest subway costs only about 10 cents). Taxi fares are also cheap: it costs only about $2-$3 to travel from the Royal Palace on Castle HIll in Buda (in West Budapest) to the Planetarium on the eastern edge of Pest. It costs about $35-$40 to hire a cab for a day-long trip.

Before going

Papers and documents

Europeans and Americans do not require a visa to visit Hungary. However, visas are required for Canadians, South Africans, Australians, New Zealanders and South Americans.

You can request a visa through a Hungarian consulate or from travel agencies by presenting a passport which is valid for at least six months. Bring along two passport pictures. The permit is good for a month's stay, but you must enter Hungary within six months.

An entrance permit may also be obtained at Ferihegy Airport, on entering the country, but there it costs more.

Young people should bring along an international youth or student certificate, even though the reductions it affords are not very large.

Those intending to drive should have a valid international driving license with them.

Insurance

Before leaving your country, don't forget to insure your luggage against damage or theft. Medical insurance is even more important, as medical treatment of any kind may be extremely expensive.

Customs regulations

The usual items that people take from one country to another may be brought into Hungary without duty: 250 cigarettes or 50 cigars, 2 liters of wine, a liter of alcohol, and personal effects. In addition to personal effects, a tourist can bring in gifts worth up to 10,000 forint (Ft.) — less than $200 — once a year. If you bring in gifts more than once a year or they are worth between 10,000 and 25,000Ft. in value, you must declare them and pay duty. A gift worth over 25,000Ft. ($450) requires a permit from the Hungarian National Bank.

Upon leaving, the tourist may take with him presents and all the belongings he brought in. Items forbidden to take out of Hungary include: food in quantities greater than what is sufficient for the journey. In particular, it is prohibited to take out sausage in amounts greater than 1 kg. This regulation is directed chiefly against Eastern European tourists, who stock up before returning to Romania or Poland, rather than against the western traveller who only wants to treat his friends to a Hungarian salami.

Advance reservations

Guide books for travellers advise reserving places in advance at the height of the tourist season on the theory that "though it may not help, it can't hurt." Experienced travellers know that in most corners of the world it is possible to manage even if arrangements are made on arrival or only a few days beforehand. In this way, you do not lose the enjoyment of freedom in making spontaneous decisions during your trip.

However, in Hungary, the situation is different. The tremendous wave of tourists (19 million tourists come to a country of 10 million inhabitants) along with the government bureaucracy, which did not encourage private enterprise to build hotels in the past, have brought about a situation where **all the hotel rooms in the main tourist centers are occupied from the beginning of May until the end of September**. It is very important to reserve hotel rooms in advance at the same time as you order airplane tickets, if you want to stay in Budapest, Sopron, Szombathely, the Balaton shores, Pécs, etc.

Those who try to find a hotel room on arrival at their destination are in for long hours of running around or waiting at the local tourist office. This fact, along with difficulties in communication for those who do not speak Hungarian, urges us to recommend unequivocally: reserve your hotel room in advance.

If you do not find the room you want (the demand for 2-4 star hotel rooms is particularly great), as often happens, it is possible to room with a family in a private home (Zimmer) — a solution which is not appropriate for some travellers, or you can take a room at a higher price in a 5-star hotel (only available in Budapest). The cost of such rooms may be a considerable burden on your budget.

Part Three — Easing the shock: where have we landed?

Getting there

By air: All flights to Hungary arrive at the Ferihegy Budapest Airport, located about 20 kms. southeast of the city. From there it is possible to get to the city center by the bus operated by *MALEV*, the Hungarian airline company or by cab. *MALEV* airline passengers arrive at Terminal No. 2, while those flying with other airlines arrive at Terminal No. 1 (for more details see heading: Budapest — How to get there).

By train: Those arriving by train undergo a short inspection and will be asked if they have Hungarian money in their possession. Only 100 forints may be brought in or taken out of the country. After your passport is stamped and you have completed the cursory customs inspection, the train continues on its way. Train passengers cannot get an entry visa at the border and must prepare it in advance. Railroad stations are located near the city centers. In the sections devoted to each city, we will explain how to get from the railroad station to the city center.

By bus: Procedures for entering the country by bus are similar to those by train, although bus passengers are sometimes asked to step out of the bus while customs inspectors search it for contraband goods.

By boat: The only practical way to enter the country by boat is, of course, via the Danube River, on a ferry boat which sails from Vienna during the tourist season. Except for the fact that boat passengers need to prepare a visa in advance, arrival procedures by boat are the same as those by air. The international platform is located in the center of Budapest, and from there, taxis and buses leave for all parts of the city.

By private car: Hungary has many border checkpoints, and most of them are open 24 hours a day, especialy those along its western border with Austria. Note that there are usually long lines at the main border crossing stations, especially the one on the Vienna-Budapest Express Highway, which are very time-consuming.

At the border station you can obtain an entrance visa without much difficulty and change your money at the bank branch or the tourist bureau on the spot. Drivers who arrive at the border without third-person insurance coverage, **mandatory** according to Hungarian law, may purchase it at the border crossing.

Domestic transportation

By air: The country is small and has no internal flights.

By train: The Hungarian railroad *(MAV)* is very efficient and pleasant for travel between the large cities. Trips are cheap, and most tourists, except back-packers and youth groups, prefer to travel first-class. Among the trains, the express (*Gyorsvonat*) or direct trains (*Sebesvonat*) are preferable, while the local trains (*Személyvonat*) should be avoided, since they are very slow and stop at every station. For most trips it is possible to purchase tickets at the railroad stations, but it's a good idea to buy them in advance at local tourist bureaus (especially *IBUSZ*) in the city center. The clerks in these bureaus speak foreign languages, unlike those in railroad stations outside Budapest.

By bus: From the bus stations, usually situated near the city center, it is possible to reach destinations near and far with the *Volán* bus company. Most of the buses are less comfortable and slower than the train; so it is recommended to travel by bus for short distances within the region you are visiting and by train for interurban travel. When clarifying departure times and prices, the Hungarian word *Autóbusz* should be used rather than the English 'bus' which has rich connotations in Hungarian, rather than denoting a many-wheeled public conveyance.

Taxis: The low cost of taxis in Hungary and their ready availability make this a highly recommended means of transportation. Most of the drivers do not speak English, so you should write down the address of your intended destination and show it to the driver, rather than trying to pronounce the name and cause the driver to shrug his shoulders uncomprehendingly. All cabs have meters and, in general, the drivers do not make unnecessary detours and overcharge, but rather try to get to your destination as quickly as possible. The price of a local taxi ride rarely goes over $2 or $3, and a cab can be hired for the day for $35-$40 or even less.

Boating: It is possible to sail the entire length of the Danube, but the only part where it is possible to go on a ferry trip is the section of the river between Budapest and Esztergom, along the Danube Bend. This trip is described later on in the section devoted to the "Bend" region.

Private car or hired: Most of the roads in Hungary are in good or even excellent condition, and driving enthusiasts will enjoy using them. In Hungary, people drive on the right side of the road. The legal speed limit in built-up areas is 60 kmh; on interurban roads, 80 kmh; on main roads, 100 kmh; and on express highways (M), 120 kmh.

The electric trams (*Villamos*) always have the right of way, and a sign saying *Kivéve Celforgalom* indicates that you are approaching a pedestrian mall where no vehicles are allowed. Drinking is forbidden when driving, and if alcohol is found in the blood of the driver, it is considered a serious offense. In case of accident, contact the police immediately by phoning 07. Those riding in the front seat must use a safety belt, and children up to age 6 are not allowed to sit in the front seat.

The Hungarian Automobile Association *MAK* offers repair service 24 hours a day for road mishaps. Call tel. 691-831 or 693-714 (in Budapest). Gas stations (*Benzin*, *Afor Benzikút*) can be found along the main roads and in the large cities. These stations sell *Normal* gasoline (86 octane), *Szuper* (92 octane), and *Extra* (98 octane). Many gas stations close at 10pm and reopen only the next morning, but there are some which stay open all night.

Car rental: It is possible to rent cars in advance at *Avis*, *Hertz*, *Europcar*, and *Budget* agencies all over the world. Despite the large supply, for those arriving during the height of the tourist season (July-August), it is important to reserve your car in advance. It is possible to rent a vehicle at the airport, at large hotels, and in many tourist bureaus. Payment for such car rentals in Hungary is accepted only in foreign currency.

Prices of car rental in Hungary are similar to those in Western Europe. If you include a trip to another country, taking the car across the border will entail a considerable additional cost. There is also an additional charge for those wishing to return the car to a station other than the one from which they rented it.

Hitch-hiking: It is difficult to hitch a ride in Hungary. The naturally suspicious nature of the Hungarians, along with the distrust of vacationers towards the young people at the side of the roads, makes such brash but charming travel quite difficult. A young woman alone has the best chance of being picked up by a passing car, but there is a certain amount of danger involved, as well as the possibility of unpleasant confrontations.

Two wheels: Hungary can be a paradise for bikers because most of it is flat land. You can travel throughout the country without much difficulty. What is difficult is to rent bikes or to find spare parts. So it is recommended that bikers come well-equipped. The motorcycle is a popular means of transport among young Austrian and West German tourists. Motorcycles have a speed limit of 80kmh on express highways and 50kmh in built-up areas. They are subject to the same laws and regulations which apply to cars.

Horseback-riding: Since the Magyars arrived in Hungary riding on their horses, their descendants continue to raise and train horses. Riding trips are organized by various tourist agencies (especially **Pegazus** at Károlyi M. utca 5 in Budapest, tel. 171-562). These trips last anywhere from several hours to a comprehensive 10-day tour throughout the country. The groups consist of 8-15 riders and an accompanying guide. The price of the trip includes the costs of food and lodging. Other trips organized by this tourist bureau are carriage tours: carriage drivers can direct their horses and wagons along the paths of the Puszta as in the Wild West.

Tourist services

Tourist agencies in Hungary serve as both information bureaus for tourists and commercial travel agencies. In every city several tourist agencies are found, each geared to a slightly different segment of the market. The long lines at such agencies are usually made up of Hungarians who come to purchase foreign currency. Be sure you are indeed waiting in the correct line to receive information.

In every city there is a local tourist agency which usually includes in its name the name of the city or region to which it belongs (e.g. *Siótour* in Siófok and *Mecsek Tourist* in Pecs). These agencies have the most reliable information on the city and events there. They also have a large listing of rooms in private homes, and offer money-changing services. This is the place to find information and services for the city and region in which you find yourself. Profits from this service go to support the city or regional government which runs the agency.

If you want information about tourist services in another city, turn to *IBUSZ*, the veteran Government Tourist Bureau. There, you can reserve hotel rooms, travel and airline tickets, organized trips, etc. all over the country. You can also exchange foreign currency for Hungarian money and can arrange for local tourist services, even though the selection is not as large as that of the local tourist agency. Clerks at *IBUSZ* are usually very busy, and do not go out of their way to supply information and answer questions of tourists. *Express* bureaus are intended to serve young tourists with limited budgets, but older back-packers can also make use of their services. The bureau also operates cheap hostels in student dormitories during school vacation and has at its disposal a number of inexpensive rooms in private homes. The *MAV* and *Volán* agencies serve mostly train and bus passengers, and they do not offer any special services for tourists.

Because of the serious competition and the increasing number of tourists, the situation is slightly different in Budapest. The excellent tourist agency *Tourinform* provides up-to-date information but does not sell tourist services. Its employees are very polite and speak many languages. Tourist services are sold by all the tourist bureaus, including private travel agencies which have sprung up recently. The largest selection is found at *IBUSZ* which operates a 24-hour-a-day service in the center of the city (for more details see the section on services for the tourist in Budapest).

Accommodation

Hungarian hotels are designated by "star" ratings as in the west. All hotels belong to the government or are jointly owned with the large world-wide hotel chains, such as the Hilton. The five-star hotels are the best but are found only in Budapest. These hotels offer all the internationally accepted modern comforts. Among the four-star hotels are some luxury hotels built at the beginning of the century for the European aristocracy. These include the *Gellért* hotel in Budapest. The two and three-star hotels are very comfortable and should not cause any concern to most tourists. When necessary, it is possible to make do with even a one-star hotel.

The scarcity of hotel rooms during the tourist season, repeatedly emphasized in this book, brought about the development of guest-houses, vacation homes, pensions, and refurbished ancient castles. The most popular category is the *Zimmer* — rooms in private homes whose rental has become a kind of national institution aimed at increasing private income which has decreased recently as a result of the economic crisis in the country. The tourist receives a key to a room in a private home which contains several beds and a closet. There is usually a common bathroom, but sometimes, the room may have a bath attached. The home-owners, who are used to this system, try to preserve their privacy and limit their contact with their guests to a minimum.

Such rooms can be arranged via different tourist bureaus or by direct contact with the locals who put up signs "Zimmer" outside their houses. Budapest home-owners who wish to rent out rooms wait for tourists either in the Budapest railroad station when trains are due from Austria or else near the *IBUSZ* office, which is open 24 hours a day.

Camping services are well-developed, and throughout the

country there are more than 100 campsites. Most are open between May and September. The campsites are categorized into four classes: in the highest class are campsites which offer full service to their guests — vacation homes, restaurant, money-changing. The lowest level of campsite includes clean, fenced-in campsites which offer only a place to put up a tent for the night. Detailed pamphlets about camping may be obtained from the tourist bureau.

Hungarian cuisine

Hungarian cuisine has developed a rich and grand tradition, beginning when the ancient Magyar tribes left the Ural steppes in order to conquer new territory more than 1,000 years ago. Enthusiasts of Hungarian cuisine claim that the smell of the meat which was then roasted beside the campfires can still be felt in the Hungarian cuisine of today — which has been enhanced over the years by absorbing Slavic, Turkish, Austrian, and French influences. Without a doubt these influences made it one of the finest kitchens on the continent. On the other hand, defamers of Hungarian cuisine claim that it is heavy, lacks delicacy, and is very conservative, having remained unchanged for over 100 years so that it lacks important elements such as fresh vegetables and fine methods of preparation. The visitor to Hungary will find evidence to support both arguments. The food is indeed rich and heavy and lacks fresh vegetables, but at times the tastefully served dishes succeed in reaching new heights of culinary excellence.

The first golden rule, which may initially appear ridiculous, but is actually quite important, is to eat the main meal at noon. The Hungarians have been doing so for hundreds of years, and the large majority of the restaurants (including luxury restaurants) prepare the food in pots during the early afternoon hours. Tourists coming to the restaurant during the late evening hours receive the food after it has spent long hours on a low flame, which has adversely affected it. The Hungarians themselves prefer to eat a cold plate of sausage or cheeses in the evening. The second rule is to limit your intake of heavy meats such as pork (*diszóhus*) and beef (*marhahús*) and look for lighter meats such as venison (*öz file*), duck (*kacsa*), rabbit (*nyúl*), or fish dishes (*halételek*).

What to eat

Salads and vegetable dishes are, as mentioned, the weak side of the meal. Lettuce salad (*tehes saláta*) is the only one which resembles salads available in the west. Most of the waiters recognize the term "mixed salad" and bring to the table a platter containing different kinds of pickled vegetables. *Alföldi Saláta*, the salad of the Puszta, does not include vegetables but rather different types of sausage in vinegar sauce. Salads containing a few fresh vegetables are usually served as a side-dish along with the main course not as a separate course.

The first course is usually soup (*leves*). The famous goulash (*gulyás*, pronounced "gu-yash") is not a main course but rather a soup which is served at the beginning of the meal. It contains pieces of beef or pork, tomatoes, green pepper, onions, paprika, etc. This soup can be a filling meal in itself and is a suitable light meal if you are not very hungry. Another tasty soup is fish soup (*halászlé*), made of fish from Lake Balaton with a large amount of paprika. This soup is right for those who like spicy foods. It is served in different variations throughout the country, and we recommend you try it in Szeged and on the shores of the Balaton. Other recommended soups are chicken soup (*ujházi tyukhusleves*) which is not spicy and contains vegetables along with the chicken. An especially rich soup is "thieves' soup" (*bakony betyárleves*) which includes chicken, beef, vegetables, noodles, and many sharp spices.

The main course is always meat which usually contains paprika and a thick gravy made with cream. *Székelygulyás*, which originated in Transylvania, is the food which most closely resembles the goulash with which we are familiar. Another version of this dish is called *bogarásgulyás*.

Additional meat dishes in gravy which are popular as main dishes are Gypsy style steak (*Ciganyrostélyos*), or rustic style (*Alföldi marharostelyos*) or *serpenyös rostéylos* — a cut of meat with potatoes and paprika. Those who prefer roasted food can order *rablóhús nyárson* in which a little bacon or mixed grill is added to the roasted meat (beef or pork). Wiener schnitzel which comes from Hungary's western neighbor is called *bécsiszelet*. With the addition of sliced cheese it is known as *Cordon Bleu*. Among the dishes prepared from poultry (*baromfi*) are chicken in paprika (*paprikás csirke*), roast duck (*sült kacsa*) and, of course the fine goose liver (*maj liba*), which is considered a special delicacy, one of the wonders of the local kitchen. The roast chicken (rántott csirke) should be avoided in most restaurants, since it is usually tough and fatty.

The lack of fresh vegetables is perhaps compensated for by vegetables stuffed with meat, such as stuffed pepper (*töltött paprika*), stuffed cabbage (*töltött káposzta*), or *erdélyi rakottk poszta* which is a delicacy made from layers of cabbage, rice, and ground meat baked together in cream.

Lake Balaton and the Danube River supply most of the fish

served. In addition to the spicy fish soup already mentioned, it is worthwhile trying the *fogas* fish served in many forms, the filled carp (*rostélyos Töltött ponty*), and the carp in cream and vegetables (*rácponty*).

The main course usually includes side dishes, but it is also possible to order: rice (*rizs*), potatoes (*metéltet*), or French fried potatoes (*sültkrumpli*), separately. For dessert the restaurants serve blini (*palacsinta*) filled with apples (*almás*) or poppy seeds (*mákos*). A tasty cold dessert is the *kompot*. Outstanding among the baked dishes is the *rétes* which the Hungarians claim is the father of the Austrian strudel and is served with different fillings, such as sliced plums (*szilvás rétes*).

Where to eat

In Hungary, you will find a restaurant on every corner. They are classified according to four levels of prices and seven different categories according to the type of food and the way it is served. It seems that in recent years the categories have become somewhat mixed, so that the categories listed below are not binding on the restaurant owners but rather serve only as a guide. A restaurant which calls itself **Restaurant** is an eating place for tourists only.

Types of restaurants

Etterem — a restaurant which serves full meals and drinks. All such restaurants must indicate the level of their prices from among the four levels and must also include a fixed menu (*Napi Menü*), which changes daily and is much cheaper than ordering each course separately.

Vendéglő — a popular restaurant which serves meals at a cheaper price than the *Etterem*.

Bisztró — a small restaurant which serves home-type cooking at low prices.

Onkiszolgáló — lowest priced restaurant with self-service.

Snackbar — a higher level of *Onkiszolgáló*.

Büfe — a snack bar serving hot and cold refreshments.

Csárda — a rustic inn with traditional atmosphere and cooking, varying from one region to another.

Cafes and patisseries

Hungary is famous throughout the culinary world for its cakes including layer cake with carmel frosting (*dobostorta*), chocolate eclairs (*kapucineres felfújt*), and many other sweets served at cafes and confectioneries. It has become de rigeur to sit and eat at such places. Along with the cup of coffee (*espresso, kávé*) the waitresses serve a glass of water and a piece of cake which you can select from the menu or point out in the window display.

Unfortunately, there has been a serious deterioration in the status and quality of cafes and the cakes they serve during the period of the Communist regime. Some of the cakes which have such a marvelous taste in neighboring Austria lose their special magic on the Hungarian side of the border (thus helping the tourist avoid temptation).

Alcoholic beverages

The fertile land and the temperate climate do wonders for the local wine (*bor*) industry, centered in Eger, Badacsony, Kecskemét, Pécs, Sopron, and the Tokaj District. Each region has its own types of wine, making an impressive array and enabling the visitor to taste a different wine at each meal and to encounter a refreshing world of tastes and colors. Among the white wines (*fehér bor*), it is worth tasting the dry wine from the Badacsony Cellars or the demi-sec *Tokaj Aszu*, considered the best wine in the country and costing a bit more. Among the red wines, we wholeheartedly recommend the light wines, such as Burgundy from the Villanyi region, and the full-bodied wines, such as the famous *Egri Bikavér*, whose name "Bull's Blood from Eger" indicates its thickness and vitality.

Besides wine, there is local beer (*sör*) or the excellent Czech Pilzner beer, as well as other good beers, imported from Austria, and thus, more expensive. Vodka enthusiasts can enjoy excellent Russian vodka which costs next to nothing. Whiskey and other imported liquor is quite expensive, and most tourists and the Hungarians settle for *Pálinka*, the local brandy manufactured in Kecskemét and in Debrecen from apricots and other fruits.

Hard liquors are available at most restaurants, but the atmosphere is particularly pleasant in the wine cellars (*Borpince*) of Eger and the other wine districts. The bars where wine (*borozó*) and beer (*sörozó*) are served are not particularly pleasant and are intended more for serious drinkers than for the average tourist.

Shopping

Hungary is famous throughout the world for its colorful village embroidery on blouses, skirts, tablecloths, etc. and for its *Herend* and *Zsolnay* porcelain which are of outstanding quality and quite ornate. Typical souvenirs also include dolls in the ancient style (produced today for tourists and not for Hungarian children), or clowns whose faces and bodies are made of fine porcelain. Other popular souvenirs are outstanding ceramic work and silver and copper items in various styles.

Hungary is a paradise for lovers of classical music. In the large cities you will find high quality, low-priced records and cassettes of classical music, gypsy music, and others. Book-lovers will find many art and photography books of excellent color and quality at surprisingly low prices.

Leather and fur coats are also a good buy in Hungary. A wealth of textile products is to be found in the shops, but they are not of very high quality and the choice of colors is limited. When buying antiques, check in advance whether it is legal to take them out of the country, in order to avoid unpleasant surprises at the border crossings.

Shopping is done at large supermarkets and at small shops in city centers such as Váci Street (Váci utca) in the center of Budapest. Because of the lack of private enterprise (until recently), the choice and prices are similar all over, so that it is preferable to make your purchases on Vaci utca at the end of your stay. Many shopkeepers here speak foreign languages.

The open and covered markets offer mostly fruits and vegetables and are of more interest to photographers than to shoppers.

Currency exchange

Forint (Ft.) is the name of the Hungarian currency. The *Forint* is divided into 100 *Fillér* (f.) The coins in use are 10, 20, and 50 *Filler* and 1, 2, 5, 10, and 20 *Forint*. The denominations of the paper money are 50, 100, 500, and 1,000 Forint. The exchange rate changes slightly every day. When changing currency, you must present your passport.

It is usually faster to change money at the tourist bureau than at a bank. Trading in foreign currency is not allowed except with banks, tourist bureaus, hotels, and at the airport. Travellers' checks, especially those of *American Express*, and credit cards such as *Eurocard* and *Diners* are accepted in Hungary in the large cities, but in rural areas, it is best to have cash on hand.

Keep the receipts you are given when you change money. Upon leaving the country you will be allowed to change 50% of your remaining Forints if they were legally purchased, but not more than $100. Changing Hungarian currency to foreign currency takes some time, so be prepared for a wait until the process is completed.

There is a thriving black market in Hungary, despite the stritct laws against it. Do not, under any circumstances, be tempted by street money changers who offer higher exchange rates per dollar; they may be undercover agents or swindlers.

General information

Working hours

In Hungary a five-day work week is the rule. Offices are open Monday through Friday, usually from 8am to 5pm, and banks from 8am to 1pm.

Shops are also supposed to be open in the morning, but most shop keepers don't open their stores before 10am, and they close at 4pm. On Thursdays most stores are open until 8 pm; on Saturday — until noon, and on Sunday, they are closed.

Museums and tourist attractions have different hours during the tourist season from the rest of the year. During the tourist season (May 1 to the end of September) most museums are open from 10am-6pm Tuesday-Sunday. During the rest of the year, many museums are closed to the public. Those which are open may be visited between 9am-7pm. Most museums and tourist sites in Hungary are closed on Mondays.

Post offices are open Monday through Friday from 8am to 5pm and on Saturdays from 8am to 1pm. Central post offices are open 7am-8pm from Monday through Saturday.

Keeping in touch

Letters: Stamps (*bélyeg*) may be purchased in tobacco shops, at reception desks in hotels and, of course, in post offices, where telegrams (*távirat*) and telexes may also be sent.

Telephone: Local telephone calls may be made from the green and yellow telephone booths found at street corners, and from those telephones painted red. It is also possible to make inter-city and international calls. Public telephones are operated with 2 Forint coins for local calls and with coins of 10, 20, and 50 Forint for inter-city and international calls. It is possible to phone abroad from the post offices, from your hotel room via the switchboard or by direct dialing.

It is not easy to get a phone connection to outside of Hungary. The prefix for international dialing is 00. International information service is available at telephone number 172-200 (Budapest area dialing code).

Newspapers: In Budapest, you will find many newspapers in English, French, and German. The Hungarian newspaper in the English language, the *Daily News*, gives the tourist interesting information about what is happening in the country, exchange rates, and a daily guide to entertainment events. This newspaper is distributed to many hotels.

Medical Services

Private and government medical services in Hungary are on quite a high level in general, but the level of treatment and the equipment vary from place to place within the country. When necessary, a private doctor is preferable to the government-sponsored service. The names of doctors, some of whom are willing to visit the sick person in his hotel room, are found at hotel reception desks. In case of emergency, dial 04 to order an ambulance.

Constant medical supervision is provided to visitors at mineral bath spas. Pharmacies (*patika* or *gyogyszertár*) are open during regular working hours and sell most of the usual medicines. There are on-duty pharmacies open 24 hours a day, particularly in Budapest. No immunizations are required to enter Hungary, and tap water is safe for drinking and bathing.

A special appendix at the end of this book is devoted to medicinal baths and dental services.

Tipping

Hungarians receive and leave tips naturally and good-naturedly. The usual tips are: for a porter — 30 Forint; for a taxi driver — 10% of the price of the trip; for a waiter — 10% of the bill; for a tour guide — 250 Forints per day; a masseur, manicurist, pedicurist — 20 Forints, to a Gypsy violinist for a special song — 100 Forints.

In case of emergency

Although the tourist should not have any special difficulties in Hungary, where the level of crime and violence is low (except, perhaps for pickpockets in crowded areas), it is advisable to know the following telephone numbers in case of emergency: police — 07, fire department — 05, ambulance — 04.

There is no special tourist police force in Hungary, and local policemen, dressed in blue-grey, very politely try to help tourists, once they have understood what is being requested of them.

Electricity; time

The electric current in the country is 220 volts. The wall plugs are the European style.

Hungarian time is one hour ahead of Greenwich time and, in summer, the clock is set ahead an additional hour.

Suggested itinerary in Hungary

A tour of Hungary will focus to a great extent on the exciting capital city Budapest. It is the place to have a good time, to shop, and to enjoy a wealth of scenic views, historic sites, as well as interesting streets and impressive buildings which have not lost their past charm. Some tourists may be satisfied with only a visit to the capital and a day-long trip to the region of the beautiful Danube Bend. But those who wish to get to know the country and its inhabitants should travel to the small towns and to the countryside.

We have divided Hungary into two geographical regions — West of the Danube River (Transdanubia) and east of it.

Transdanubia is the more interesting of the two regions. From Budapest, we turn west to Győr and to northwest Hungary. From there, we continue on to Lake Balaton, and after relaxing along its shores, we continue southward to Pécs and to southern Transdanubia. The visit to western Hungary will end with a return to Budapest.

Those who still have some time to spend in Hungary can go to the regions which are east of the Danube: to the Great Plain — to Kecskemét, Szeged, and Debrecen, or to the mountains in the north — to Eger, the Tokaj region, and the Aggtelek Caves.

HUNGARY

Budapest

Budapest is not only the official capital of Hungary. It is fair to describe it as the heart, mind, and nerve center of the Magyar people. Budapest is a beautiful city, one of the most splendid cities in Europe. It has over 2,000,000 inhabitants, one fifth of the country's total population.

Budapest is actually a group of cities which includes Óbuda, Buda, and Pest. It is spread across both sides of the Danube and contains a wealth of luxurious palaces, impressive public buildings, wide boulevards, green parks, an extensive cultural life and excellent restaurants. Pest is located on the river plain, while Buda lies on pleasant hillsides, which adds a dramatic dimension to the beauty of the city.

A visit to Budapest should not be limited to one or two days. The many sites and scenic landscapes justify a stay of several days. In addition to the city's sites, one-day excursions can be planned to the hills of Buda, the Danube Bend, and other places as well.

Budapest is the delightful jewel of Hungary, and was always considered as "the showcase of the Eastern bloc." In its concert halls performances take place of classical music, opera, and theater. The shops offer an amazing abundance of products not to be found at other places in Eastern Europe, and in its main streets, the young men and women are seen wearing modern dress with up-to-date hairstyles. Undoubtedly, the visit to Budapest constitutes the highpoint of the Hungarian trip. The city which is nicknamed "the Paris of Eastern Europe" deserves this appellation — it is the pride of all the country's citizens because of its beauty and its vitality.

History of the city

Archeological findings reveal that settlement in the area of Budapest began during the pre-historical period. The

HUNGARY

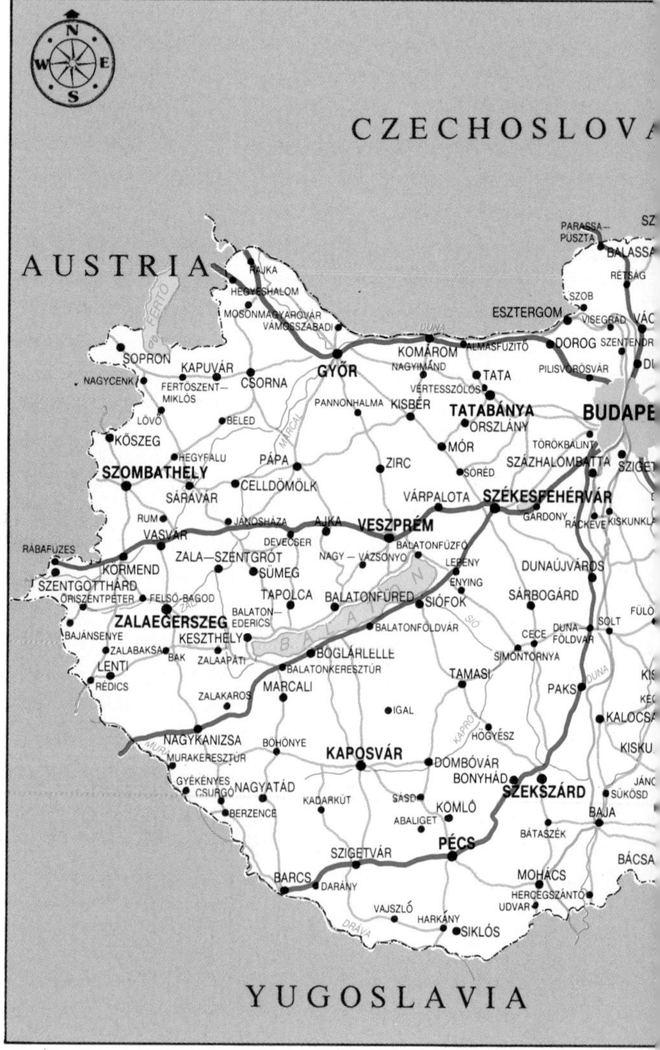
N
W
E
S
AUSTRIA
YUGOSLAVIA
RAJKA
HEGYESHALOM
MOSONMAGYARÓVÁR
VÁMOSSZABADI
FERTŐ
DUNA
SOPRON
NAGYCENK
KAPUVÁR
FERTŐSZENT-MIKLÓS
CSORNA
GYŐR
KOMÁROM
ALMÁSFÜZITŐ
NAGYIGMÁND
VÉRTESSZŐLŐS
TATA
PANNONHALMA
KISBÉR
TATABÁNYA
ORSZLÁNY
MÓR
ZIRC
SÓRÉD
LÖVŐ
BELED
KŐSZEG
HEGYFALU
SZOMBATHELY
SÁRVÁR
PÁPA
CELLDÖMÖLK
MARCAL
VÁRPALOTA
SZÉKESFEHÉRVÁR
GÁRDONY
RÁCKEVE
SZÁZHALOMBATTA
TÖRÖKBÁLINT
ESZTERGOM
SZOB
VISEGRÁD
DOROG
PILISVÖRÖSVÁR
PARASSA-PUSZTA
RÉTSÁG
RUM
VASVÁR
JÁNOSHÁZA
AJKA
VESZPRÉM
DEVECSER
RÁBAFÜZES
KÖRMEND
ZALA—SZENTGRÓT
SÜMEG
NAGY — VÁZSONY
BALATONFÜZFŐ
LEPENY
ENYING
DUNAÚJVÁROS
SZENTGOTTHÁRD
ŐRISZENTPÉTER
FELSŐ-BAGOD
TAPOLCA
BALATONFÜRED
SIÓFOK
SÁRBOGÁRD
ZALAEGERSZEG
BALATON-EDERICS
BALATONFÖLDVÁR
BALATON
SIÓ
BAJÁNSENYE
KESZTHELY
CECE
DUNA-FÖLDVÁR
SOLT
ZALABAKSA
BAK
ZALAAPÁTI
BOGLÁRLELLE
SIMONTORNYA
LENTI
BALATONKERESZTÚR
TAMÁSI
RÉDICS
ZALAKAROS
MARCALI
PAKS
IGAL
KAPOS
HŐGYÉSZ
NAGYKANIZSA
MURA
BÖHÖNYE
KAPOSVÁR
MURAKERESZTÚR
DOMBÓVÁR
BONYHÁD
SZEKSZÁRD
GYÉKÉNYES
CSURGÓ
NAGYATÁD
KADARKÚT
SÁSD
KOMLÓ
ABALIGET
BERZENCE
BAJA
SÜKÖSD
BÁTASZÉK
SZIGETVÁR
PÉCS
MOHÁCS
BARCS
DARÁNY
HERCEGSZÁNTÓ
UDVAR
VAJSZLÓ
HARKÁNY
SIKLÓS
DRÁVA

HUNGARY

U. S. S. R.
ROMANIA
TORNANÁDASKA
TORNYOSNÉMETI
SÁTORALJAÚJHELY
AGGTELEK
EDELÉNY
ENCS
SÁROSPATAK
BÁNRÉVE
PUTNOK
KAZINCBARCIKA
CIGÁND
KISVÁRDA
SORHÁZ U.
ÓZD
DOMBRÁD
BEREGSURÁNY
TISZABECS
TOKAJ
SZILVÁSVÁRAD
MISKOLC
SZERENCS
RAKAMAZ
NYÍRBOGDÁNY
VÁSÁROSNAMÉNY
FEHÉRGYARMAT
TARNALELESZ
TISZA-
VASVÁRI
NYÍREGYHÁZA
VAJA
BÁTONYTERENYE
NYÉKLÁDHÁZA
EGER
LENINVÁROS
MÁTÉSZALKA
PARÁD
HAJDÚNÁNÁS
ÁGERDŐMAJOR
CSENGERSIMA
MEZŐKÖVESD
POLGÁR
KERECSEND
NYÍRBÁTOR
VALLAJ
GYÖNGYÖS
FÜZESABONY
HAJDÚBÖSZÖRMÉNY
KÁPOLNA
NYÍRADONY
DORMÁND
TISZAFÜRED
HEVES
KISKÖREI
VIZTÁROLÓ
HORTOBÁGY
DEBRECEN
NYÍRÁBRÁNY
JÁSZAPÁTI
HAJDÚSZOBOSZLÓ
VÁMOSPÉRCS
KUNMADARAS
ÚJSZÁSZ
BERKEKFÜRDŐ
PÜSPÖKLADÁNY
BERETTYÓÚJFALU
BIHAR-
KERESZTES
ABONY
TÖRÖKZENTMIKÓS
KISÚJSZÁLLAS
FURTA
SZOLNOK
TÜRKEVE
ÁRTÁND
DÉVAVÁNYA
TISZAKÉCSKE
TISZAFÖLDVÁR
MEZŐTÚR
SZEGHALOM
KOMÁDI
GYOMAENDRŐD
KÖRÖSLADÁNY
SZARVAS
KUN-
SZENTMÁRTON
BÉKÉS
SARKAD
BÉKÉSCSABA
KÖTEGYÁN
CSONGRÁD
SZENTES
GYULA
OROSHÁZA
HÓDMEZŐVÁSÁRHELY
TÓTKOMLÓS
LŐKÖSHÁZA
MEZŐKOVÁCSHÁZA
MEZŐHEGYES
DOMBEGYHÁZ
SZEGED
MAROS
MAKÓ
TISZA
SAJÓ
HERNÁD
BODROG
TARNA
KÖRÖS
BERETTYÓ
SZAMOS
KM
0
25
50
MILES
0
25
50

first permanent settlement here was a stronghold which apparently was founded in the 4th century BC by Celtic tribes who controlled the area. The stronghold was called Ak-ink, meaning "abundant water" and was established in the region of what is today Gellért.

The Romans, who came following the Celts in the 1st century AD, built a large army camp at the bend of the Danube for their legionnaires. The camp grew and served as a base for the Roman soldiers who were stationed all along the Danube — the boundary of the Roman Empire at that time. The number of soldiers is estimated to have been 20,000 or more. In the city, which was established alongside the army camp, dwelt merchants and tradesmen whose income came mostly from the soldiers. The Romans used the ancient Celtic name and called the new city Aquincum. It expanded from the direction of Obuda to the area of what is Buda today.

In the year 106 AD, Aquincum became the capital of the Roman province of Lower Pannonia. A huge stadium was built, as well as baths and public buildings. At its high point, Aquincum had 100,000 inhabitants — a large number for those times. In order to defend themselves from invasions from the east, the Romans built a stronghold on the other side of the Danube in the 3rd century. The walled fortress was called Contra Aquincum, and it was the predecessor of what is Pest today.

The Hun invaders conquered Aquincum at the beginning of the 5th century AD, and the Roman city lost its importance for a period of several centuries. The first Magyar kings, who conquered the country and established a Christian monarchy in the 11th century, prefered the cities of Esztergom and Székesfehérvár. It was only in the middle of the 13th century that Aquincum was revived, when King Béla IV established the fortress city of **Vár hegy** on Castle Hill in order to defend the old city of Buda (Obuda) against the Mongols. Along with the military construction, the city also developed into a center of commerce and of religious institutions (the monastery on Margit Island, the **Belvarosi** Church in Pest). Sigismund of the House of Luxembourg, ruler of Hungary, started to build a Gothic style palace on Castle Hill at the beginning of the 15th century. Under the rule of Matthias Corvinus, in the second half of the 15th century, Buda served as the center of government in Hungary. King Matthias beautified and expanded the royal palace in Italian Renaissance style and made it the seat of government. At the same time, Pest became a popular center for merchants, craftsmen and others who served the aristocracy in Buda.

Hungarian kings ruled in Buda until the Turkish conquest in 1541. The Turks did not destroy the city. They left their architectural imprint in the form of beautiful mosques. At the end of the 17th century, after lengthy battles which caused death and destruction in Buda, the Turks were forced out. Most of the inhabitants either fled or were killed. Under the new Hapsburg rulers, Budapest again flourished with the aid of German, Slovakian, and Serbian immigrants along with the Hungarians who returned. Monumental buildings were constructed in the Baroque style typical of the period.

The city's development gathered momentum in the first half of the 19th century. The central figure responsible was the regent Istvan Széchenyi who undertook, among other things, the planning of the first permanent bridge between Buda and Pest, which is named after him (**Széchenyi híd**). The purpose of the bridge was to connect Óbuda, Buda, and Pest.

And indeed, in 1873, Óbuda, Buda, and Pest were united into one city. The resulting city of Budapest had over 300,000 inhabitants and was declared the capital of Hungary. This was a period of building and progress during which the city expanded and many buildings were constructed: in Hungarian romantic style — the concert hall of Pest (Vigadó); and in neo-Gothic style — the impressive parliament building. It was actually this period which determined the character and appearance of the city as we know it today.

The end of the First World War and the fall of the House of Hapsburg brought to power Admiral Miklós Horthy who made the royal palace in Buda his seat of government. He concluded a pact with the Nazis during the Second World War and ruled by their sufferance until they forced him out in 1944. The Red Army fought to conquer Budapest during the last year of the Second World War. In the fierce fighting that took place, many of the buildings were completely destroyed, and most other structures and bridges were damaged. At the height of the battle, the fighting spread into the city, and eyewitnesses claim that the frozen Danube changed its color from snowy white to red from the blood of both soldiers and civilians. The final liberation by the Russians took place in February 1945.

In the period after the war, the city experienced extensive

Erzsébet Bridge

The Citadel on Gellért Hill

reconstruction. Under the communist government, the city's buildings including the Royal Palace, were restored and renovated. The city was virtually rebuilt, meticulously and precisely, yet the visitor to Castle Hill can still see the scars from bullets and shells from the war. After the war, memorial monuments were erected, such as the Freedom Monument on Gellért Hill, in addition to stadiums and public parks. The city was enhanced by a surrounding ring of large residential neighborhoods — the contribution of socialist architecture — which has given Budapest its present form.

Geographical location

Budapest is located on both sides of the Danube — Buda lies on the western hills, and Pest is built on the plain east of the wide river. Seven bridges connect the two parts of the city. The island of Margit (Margit Sziget), an amusement and vacation park on the Danube in the north of the city, is connected to both Buda and Pest by Arpad Bridge (Arpád híd) — the northernmost bridge, and by Margit Bridge (Margit híd).

Óbuda, the old part of Buda, is north of Buda and contains the remains of the Roman city of Aquincum. In **Buda**, apparently named after the brother of Attila the Hun, are two high hills: Castle Hill (Várhegy), the site of the royal palace, and Gellért Hill (Gellért Hegy), where the Citadel and the Liberation Monument (Felszabadul si Emlekmü) are found. From the Citadel and the Monument there is a marvelous view of this beautiful city.

Flat **Pest** was built up as a defense fortification for the Roman stronghold in Buda and Óbuda. The inner core of the city (*Belvaros*), surrounded by the József Attila, Tanács, Múzeum, and Vamház Boulevards, corresponds to the site of the ancient Roman position. These boulevards are called the "small boulevards" (*Kis körút*). The area is served by the Szécheny, Erzsébet, and Zsabadság bridges. About 150 years ago, an additional wide belt developed around the center, enclosed by the "great boulevards" (*Nagy körút*) — Szt. István, Teréz, Erzsébet, József, and Ferenz Boulevards — which are connected to Buda by the Petőfi and the Margit bridges.

Pest contains the thriving business center of the Hungarian capital. This is the lively, colorful part of the city, with cultural centers, shopping centers, and large hotels. The many residential buildings and housing projects beyond the great boulevards are less interesting and impressive and do not attract many tourists.

How to get there

By air

All flights to Hungary arrive at Ferihegy Airport, located about 20 kms southeast of the city center. Terminal 1 is older and serves passengers of most foreign airlines who arrive in Budapest. Terminal 2, modern and spacious, is located 4 kms beyond the first terminal and serves passengers of *MALEV* and a few other airlines. In future it will serve most passenger flights. In both terminals entrance permits for Hungary are available. Cars may be hired at one of the car rental agencies at both of the terminals (*Hertz, Avis, Budget, Europcar*), and reservations for hotel rooms can be made at the tourist bureau.

Every 30 minutes a bus leaves the airport for Erzsébet Square (Erzsébet tér) in the city center, where the central bus station is also located. Busses run continuously between 6am-10pm, the trip takes about 30 minutes and costs less than a dollar. Tickets may be bought on the bus. A trip by taxi from the airport to the city takes about 20 minutes.

By boat

From April 1 until October 1 a hydrofoil service operates along the 282 kms of the Danube between Vienna and Budapest. The boat trip on the Danube takes 4.5 hours.

The hydrofoil anchors at the international harbor in Pest along Belgrade Dock (Nemzetközi Hajoállomás Belgrád Rakpart). You can get information about departures and purchase tickets in *IBUSZ* offices in Vienna (tel. 51-55-50) and in Budapest (tel. 142-3410), or at the *Mahart* boat company offices at the boat dock in Budapest (tel. 118-1953) and in Vienna (tel. 505-3844).

From May through about mid-September there are daily departures from Vienna at 2:30pm which arrive in the evening in Budapest. At the height of the season — June 6 to September 9 — an additional hydrofoil is put into operation, leaving Vienna in the mornings. During April and during the second half of September the hydrofoil leaves Vienna at 8am, arriving in Budapest around noon. Sailing times and frequency of service from Budapest to Vienna are similar.

By train
Budapest has good connections with the other large Hungarian and European cities. About 30 international railroad lines connect it with various destinations. The most popular lines are from Vienna (4 hrs.), Zagreb (6 hrs.), Frankfurt (15 hrs.), and Paris (21 hrs.). Travellers holding *InterRail* and *Euro-Train* tickets receive reductions of up to 50% on train fares in Hungary. *Eurail Pass* holders are entitled to free train rides inside Hungary. Young people under 26 years of age, students, and pensioners also receive reductions.

Budapest has three main train stations (*pályaudvar*). The eastern station (Keleti pu.), the western station (Nyugati pu.) — both in Pest; and the southern station (Déli pu.) in Buda. These stations are a lively center for transportation and shopping between 6am-8pm. On the lower level are the subway stations, providing quick connections to most parts of the city. Outside the station are bus stops and taxi stands. Loading carts are available at the stations to serve the passengers, and, for a modest tip, polite porters will take your luggage straight to your waiting taxi.

Train passengers from Western Europe usually arrive at the eastern station (Keleti pályaudvar) in Pest. Local residents who have rooms to rent often await tourists arriving at this station and try to persuade them to rent a room in their home. Keep a map of the city handy so that you can ask the landlord to point out the location of his house and the connections it has by taxi, busses and subway with the city center.

Remember that train passengers must arrive at border crossings with a visa already stamped in their passport.

By bus
A number of international bus lines connect Budapest to the other cities of Europe. The most popular line is from Vienna (4hrs, $22). Busses also come from Munich, Venice, Helsinki, Warsaw, London, etc. For details and for departure times: Vienna — tel. 51-55-50; Munich — tel. 265-020; Venice — tel. 52-38-112; Ljubljana — tel. 31-221, and London — tel. 730-0202.

Bus travel inside Hungary is quite slow since the busses stop at many stations in the villages and towns along the way. For trips lasting over an hour, it is preferable to go by train. This is especially the case for international trips, which can prove

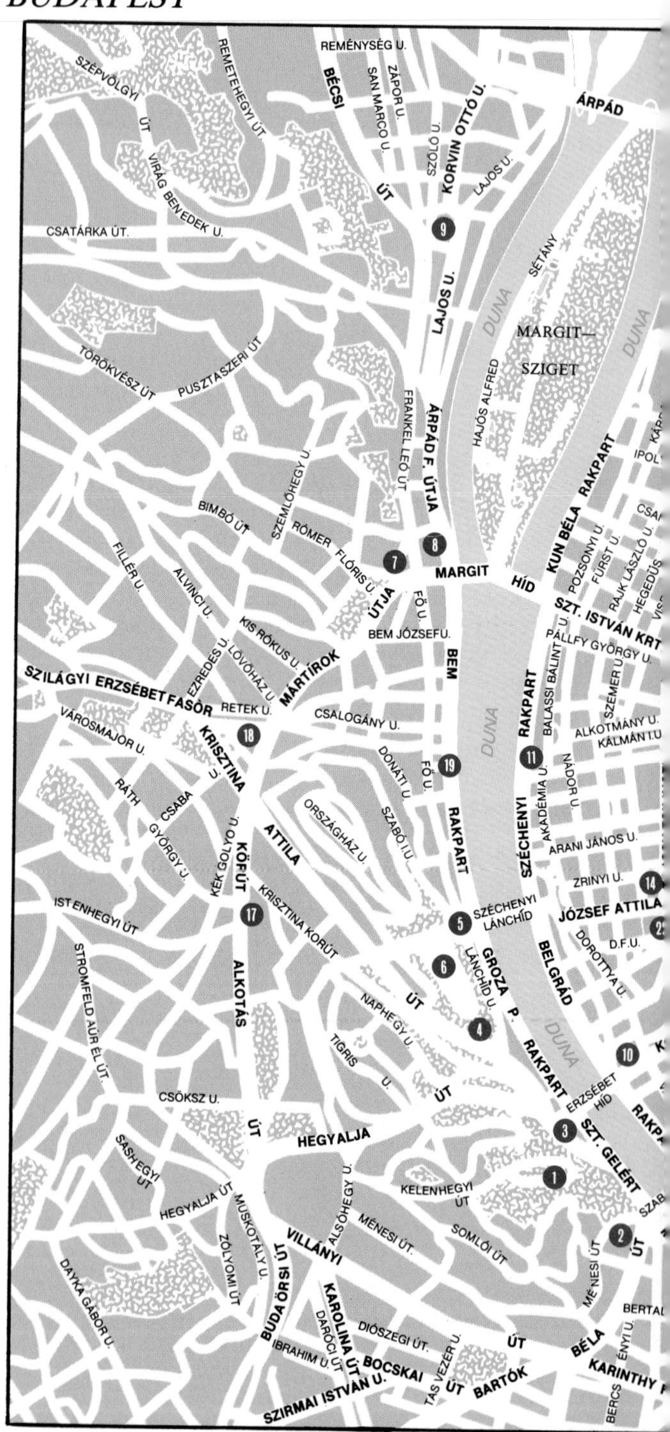
REMÉNYSÉG U.
BÉCSI
ZÁPOR U.
SAN MARCO U.
SZÖLŐ U.
KORVIN OTTÓ U.
ÁRPÁD
LAJOS U.
ÚT
REMETEHEGYI ÚT
SZÉPVÖLGYI
ÚT
VIRÁG BENEDEK U.
CSATÁRKA ÚT
LAJOS U.
SÉTÁNY
DUNA
MARGIT—
SZIGET
DUNA
TÖRÖKVÉSZ ÚT
PUSZTASZERI ÚT
FRANKEL LEÓ ÚT
ÁRPÁD F. ÚTJA
HAJÓS ALFRED
SZEMLŐHEGY U.
BIMBÓ ÚT
RÓMER
FLÓRIS U.
ÚTJA
MARGIT
HÍD
KUN BÉLA
RAKPART
IPOLY
POZSONYI U.
FÜRST U.
RAJK LÁSZLÓ U.
HEGEDŰS
SZT. ISTVÁN KRT
FILLÉR U.
ALVINCI U.
KIS RÓKUS U.
FŐ U.
BEM JÓZSEF U.
BEM
PÁLLFY GYÖRGY U.
EZREDES U.
LÖVŐHÁZ U.
MÁRTÍROK
SZILÁGYI ERZSÉBET FASOR
RETEK U.
CSALOGÁNY U.
BALASSI BÁLINT U.
RAKPART
SZEMERE U.
ALKOTMÁNY U.
KÁLMÁN I.U.
VÁROSMAJOR U.
KRISZTINA
DONÁTI U.
DUNA
RÁTH
CSABA
GYÖRGY U.
ATTILA
ORSZÁGHÁZ U.
SZABÓ I.U.
FŐ U.
RAKPART
SZÉCHENYI
AKADÉMIA U.
NÁDOR U.
ARANI JÁNOS U.
ZRINYI U.
KÉK GOLYÓ U.
KŐFÚT
KRISZTINA KORÚT
ISTENHEGYI ÚT
SZÉCHENYI LÁNCHÍD
JÓZSEF ATTILA
DOROTTYA U.
D.F.U.
STROMFELD AÚR ÉL ÚT
ALKOTÁS
ÚT
NAPHEGY U.
LÁNCHÍD U.
GROZA P.
BELGRÁD
TIGRIS
U.
DUNA
RAKPART
ÚT
CSÖKSZ U.
ERZSÉBET HÍD
ÚT
HEGYALJA
SZT. GELÉRT
SASHEGYI ÚT
KELENHEGYI ÚT
ALSÓHEGY U.
HEGYALJA ÚT
MUSKOTÁLY U.
MÉNESI ÚT
SOMLÓI ÚT
VILLÁNYI
ZÓLYOMI ÚT
MÉNESI ÚT
ÚT
DAYKA GÁBOR U.
BUDAÖRSI ÚT
KAROLINA ÚT
DARÓCI ÚT
IBRAHIM U.
DIÓSZEGI ÚT
BOCSKAI
TAS VEZÉR U.
ÚT
BÉLA
ÚT
BARTÓK
SZIRMAI ISTVÁN U.
KARINTHY
BERCS
ÉNYI U.
9
8
7
18
19
11
14
17
5
6
4
10
3
1
2

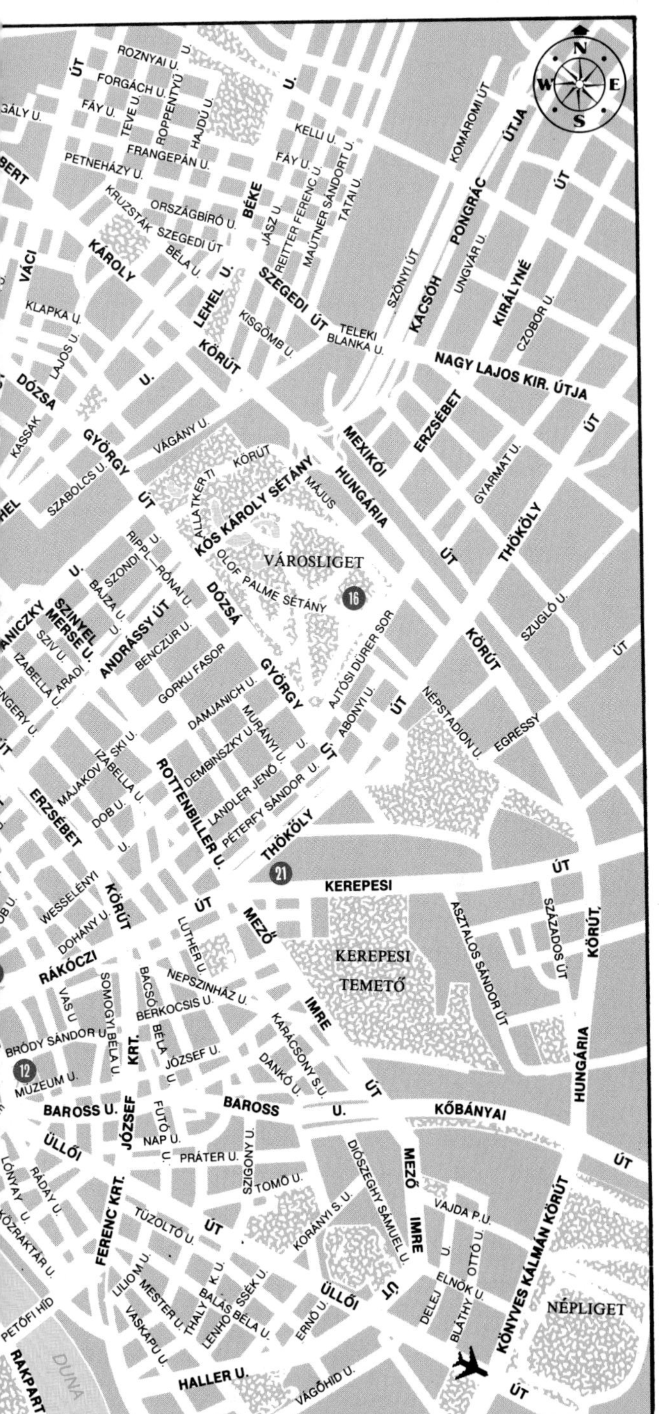

VÁROSLIGET
KEREPESI TEMETŐ
NÉPLIGET
DUNA
KŐS KÁROLY SÉTÁNY
OLOF PALME SÉTÁNY
NAGY LAJOS KIR. ÚTJA
KEREPESI
KŐBÁNYAI
KÖNYVES KÁLMÁN KÖRÚT
HUNGÁRIA KÖRÚT
ANDRÁSSY ÚT
RÁKÓCZI
BAROSS U.
ÜLLŐI
THÖKÖLY
MEXIKÓI
DÓZSA GYÖRGY ÚT

very tiring by bus. Most busses arrive and depart from the central terminal in Erzsébet tér in the center of Pest.

By car

Most of the roads to Budapest are pleasant and in good repair. From Lake Balaton, E71 takes you to Budapest and continues on to Miskolc. From Vina and Győr, E60 passes through and continues on to Debrecen. Road E73 and highway 6, reach Budapest from the Yugoslavian border in the south. Road E75, connects Szeged and Budapest. To leave for Poland in the north, take road E77. Distances from Budapest to the main cities in Hungary are short, since Budapest is located in the center of the country.

The closest major international destination is Vienna, 248 kms. away. Other nearby cities include Belgrade (394 kms.), Munich (691 kms.), Warsaw (709 kms.), and Bucharest (830 kms.). On arrival in Budapest, follow the signs which say *Centrum* in order to get to the center of the city.

Tourist services

Many of the tourist information bureaus in Budapest are actually travel agencies which distribute government and private publications to tourists. The government tourist company *IBUSZ* operates several branches in the city. It is the leading company in organizing sleeping accommodations and trips. Other agencies in the city, such as *Cooptourist*, offer a large selection of rooms in private homes and a smaller selection of hotel rooms.

Index

1. Gellért Hill
2. Gellért Hotel
3. Rudas Bath-House
4. Semmelweis Museum
5. Adam Clark Square
6. Castle Hill
7. Gul Baba Tomb
8. Lukács Bath House
9. Roman Amphitheatre
10. City Parish church
11. Parliament
12. National Museum
13. Old Synagogue
14. The Great Basilica
15. Opera House
16. City Park
17. Dély railway station
18. Moscow Square bus station
19. Batthyany Square Suburbs train station
20. Nyugati railway station
21. Keleti railway station
22. Erzsébet Square bus station

A tourist seeking information only would do best to inquire at *Tourinform* near Deák tér (2 Sütő utca, tel. 117-9800), which is open Mon.-Sat. from 8am-8pm and on Sundays 8am-1pm. The staff speaks several languages and cheerfully provides a wealth of information about the Hungarian capital and the possibilities for side trips and entertainment in it, as well as about Hungary in general.

A tourist wishing to reserve a room or arrange a trip in the city or in its vicinity should turn to the main *IBUSZ* office (3c Tanács körút, tel. 121-1007) or to one of its other branches in the city, such as the branch which offers help in finding sleeping accommodations for tourists 24 hours a day (3 Petőfi tér, tel. 118-5707). Rooms in private homes can be had at low prices.

The *Express* agency specializes in services for young people and has offices in the large railroad stations and at 16 Szabadsag tér (tel. 131-3517).

Post offices in the Nyugati railroad station (Teréz körút) and in the Keleti station (Baross tér) are open 24 hours a day. From these post offices you can make international telephone calls and send letters and packages. Poste Restante is located at 13 Petőfi utca (open Mon.-Fri. 8am-6pm and on Saturdays 8am-2pm). You can buy postage stamps at post offices, large hotels, and in stores. Letters sent to *American Express* are usually held for the visitor at the *IBUSZ* office which is open 24 hours a day. When sending a letter to Hungary, write the surname first, as is the practice there.

Local transportation

The best way to get know this charming city is to walk around its beautiful streets. However, because of its size and the distances between certain landmarks, it is also necessary to make use of municipal public transportation. The **subway** (*Metro*) is comfortable, convenient, and cheap. It has three lines which all meet in the center of Pest, at the Deák tér Station. Line 1 (marked in yellow) leads northeast from Vörösmarty Square via the Opera House to Mexikő Street. Line 2 (marked in red) connects the Déli train station in Buda with Ors vezér tér in eastern Pest via the center of the city and the Keleti train station. Line 3 (marked in blue) starts at Arpád Bridge, goes along the Danube, and then to the Kispest Quarter at the southern end of the city.

Pest railway station

The Metro operates daily from 4:30am-11pm. Trains come often and are clean and well-lit. Tickets should be bought before entering the train at the ticket booths (*Cassa*), and should be stamped at the automat in the entrance hall. The ticket booths are often closed, so we suggest you buy a number of tickets in advance or else stock up on 2 Forint and 5 Forint coins which can be used to buy your tickets in the automatic dispenser. If you are stuck with no tickets and no coins, you can buy tickets from inspectors who are found in a special room with the word *Informacio* or the letter *i* alone written over the door. Tickets are only valid for one hour after being stamped and can be used on one line only.

Those preferring to travel above ground can take the **bus** (*autobusz*), trolley (*trolibusz*), or tram (*villamos*). The latter two operate on electricity; the trolley-bus is a bus connected to an overhead electric cable, while the tram travels on tracks. These busses and streetcars cover the city in an efficient transportation network. The price of a trip via this means of travel is very cheap and differs according to the destination. Children up to age 6 ride free. Tickets must be purchased before boarding.

You can buy a day-pass (*Napijegy*) at the ticket booths, valid for local travel, which costs about $1. You can also purchase a monthly-pass ticket which requires a passport picture and costs only about $3. This ticket is valid for a month of trips on all municipal transport, from the date of purchase until the fifth day of the following month. The ticket may be purchased at *Metro* and train stations.

The **suburban train** (*HEV*) leaves every few minutes from Batthyány tér in Buda, travelling north for 30 minutes, traversing the northern suburbs Aquincum and Pomáz, and terminating at Szentendre.

Sufficient **taxis** (*Taxi*) are available, and the fares are quite cheap. Taxis can be ordered from the *Főtaxi* office, tel. 118-8888. In addition to the government-owned taxis, there are also private cabs, but their prices are likely to be high.

Car rental

Cars should be ordered before arrival, because the demand is much greater than the supply. Cars of various makers can be rented, from the small, cheap Russian Lada to modern, air-conditioned BMWs. International companies are represented by the large tourist agencies.

Avis: 8 Martinelli tér, tel. 118-6222 (represented by *IBUSZ*).
Europcar: 16 Vaskapú utca, tel. 133-4783 (represented by *Volán*).
Hertz: 24 Kertész utca, tel. 111-6116 (represented by *Főtaxi*).
Budget: 15 Kossuth tér, tel. 111-8803 (represented by *Cooptourist*).

Accommodation

The shortage of hotels throughout Hungary is most in evidence in Budapest during the tourist season: for weeks at a time it is impossible to find an empty hotel room in the city, and tourists arriving without having made advance reservations need to choose between sleeping in a room in a private home or in a luxury hotel (costing over $150 per night), which are often also unavailable. In spring and autumn, it is also difficult to find an empty room, and even in winter, you may discover that your first choice of hotel has no room available. Therefore, **reserve rooms in advance!**

Types of accommodation vary greatly: hotels, classified by the number of stars; pensions; rooms in private houses; and cheap hostels, mostly on university campuses during school vacation.

Luxury hotels (5 stars)

Hilton: 1-3 Hess András tér (tel. 175-1000, telex 22-5984). In addition to all the amenities which characterize the international hotel chain, this hotel is notable for its marvelous view, because of its location beside Matthias Church on Castle Hill in Buda. The hotel has a casino, a night club, and...the remains of a 13th century church which were integrated into the hotel's construction. Even if you don't intend to stay at the hotel, it is worth a visit.

Thermal: Margitsziget (tel. 132-1100, telex 22-5463). Located on Margit Island, it specializes in various medicinal treatments combined with massage, acupuncture, and thermal baths.

Atrium Hyatt: 2 Roosevelt tér (tel. 138-3000, telex 22-5485). This luxury hotel is located alongside the Danube River and is run by the international *Hyatt* chain. Many consider it the best hotel in town, even though its prices are lower than the *Hilton*.

Duna Intercontinental: 4 Apáczai Csere János utca (tel. 117-5122, telex 22-5277). This is another prestigious hotel location (close to *Atrium Hyatt)*, rooms facing the Danube. required services.

High-priced hotels (4 stars)

Forum: Apáczai Csere Janos utca (tel. 111-78088). Good location (close to the Atrium Hyatt), rooms facing the Danube.

Gellért: 1 Gellért tér (tel. 185-2200, telex. 22-4363), built after World War I in the art noveau style, is a landmark which retains the flavor of the past and is very elegant. The hotel is located at the foot of Gellért Hill in Buda and offers thermal baths, a Turkish bath, and a swimming pool considered the cleanest and most beautiful in the city. Arrangements can be made to use these facilities even if you are not staying at the hotel (there is an entrance fee).

Béke: 97 Teréz körút (tel. 132-3300, telex 22-5748). This is one of the older hotels which has been tastefully renovated, located beside Marx tér in Pest. Among other things, it is

noted for its famous night club, the *Orfeum*.
Ramada Grand: on Margit Island (tel. 111-1000, telex 22-6682), first opened in 1873 (without the name *Ramada*, of course), it served the Hungarian and European aristocracy who came on vacation to the thermal springs of Margit Island. The hotel was closed for renovation, reopening in 1987, equipped with all the modern conveniences. Still, something of its former grandeur was lost.
Novotel: 63-67 Alkotás utca (tel. 186-9588, telex 22-5496). This is a modern, expensive, up-to-date hotel. It is comfortable but lacks style. In Buda, a bit distant from the center of action.

Moderate hotels (2-3 stars)

Erzsébet: Ferenciek tér, 11-15 Károly Mihály utca (tel. 138-2111). For those who like old renovated hotels.
Metropol: 58 Rákóczi út (tel. 142-1175). It, too, is an old hotel, but somewhat gloomy.
Astoria: 19 Kossuth Lajos utca (tel. 117-3411).
Medosz: 9 Jókai tér (tel. 153-1700). A pleasant hotel in a convenient location, its price is among the lowest in this category.
Kőnyves: 44 Kőnyves Kálmán körút (tel. 133-6057). While this hotel is far from the center of town, its proximity to a subway station and its proprietor, who supplies a wealth of information about the life of the city and its secrets, make a stay here most pleasant. This is the most outstanding hotel in the new hotel chain, *Epitőipari Szolgáltató*.
Vállalat: Seven hotels, including three which are 2-star. This hotel chain started with rooming houses which were intended as sleeping quarters for workers from outside the city. The rooms were quickly renovated in order to meet the demand for the growing wave of tourists. Apparently, clerks at *IBUSZ* are not too well-informed about details concerning this chain. Additional information is available at the offices of the management (*Bartók Hotel* in Buda, 152 Bartók Béla, tel. 185-1188, telex 22-6089).

Inexpensive hotels (1 star hotels, pensions, and hostels)

Citadella: In the old fortress on Gellért Hill (tel. 166-5794). The most outstanding of the inexpensive hotels in the city, it has one star. From its windows, an exciting view of the city stretches before you. The place is quite noisy because

of the many young people from Central and Eastern Europe who stay here!
Express: 7-9 Beethoven utca (tel. 175-3082). Run by the *Express* agency, which operates pensions and hostels for young people, mostly in university dormitories during the summer vacation of the students.

Private rooms (Zimmer)

In Budapest a most acceptable way to overcome the shortage of hotel rooms is to stay in a private home with a local family. It is possible to rent such a room through any of the tourist agencies in the city (the largest selection is at the *IBUSZ* agency) or else privately: local residents wait for tourists in the Keleti train station when trains arrive from Western Europe and next to *IBUSZ*, opposite the *Intercontinental* hotel.

If you reserve a room through the services of a tourist agency, you must pay in foreign currency; if you make a private arrangement, you can pay in Hungarian currency.

Restaurants

Luxury restaurants

In the luxury restaurants of Budapest there is a pleasant atmosphere replete with the elegance of bygone days. In the evenings, the food is served to the accompaniment of a Hungarian or Gypsy orchestra. Formal dress is necessary, and it is recommended to reserve places in advance.

In Buda

Alabárdos: 2 Országház utca (tel. 156-0851). Considered the best restaurant in Budapest.
Aranyhordó: 16 Tárnok utca (tel. 156-6765). A popular restaurant serving Hungarian and international cuisine.
Régi Országház: 17 Országház utca (tel. 175-0650).

In Pest

Gundel: 2 Allatkerti utca (tel. 122-1002). One of the best restaurants in the city.
Hungária: 9-11 Teréz körút (tel. 122-3849). Opened in 1894 as the *New-York*, it was destroyed during the Second World War and faithfully rebuilt. The food is less impressive than the decor.

Good restaurants (moderately-priced)

Kacsa: 75 Fő utca (tel. 135-3357). In Buda. Highly recommended.
Fehér Galamb: Alongside Matthias Church on Castle Hill (tel. 175-6975). Highly recommended. It offers Gypsy music.
Megyeri Csárda: 102 Váci utca. Known for its excellent musicians.
Aposto: 4-6 Kigyo utca (tel. 118-3704). Its food does not live up to its advertising.
Múzeum: Next to the National Museum (tel. 113-8282).
Vigadó: In the concert hall of the same name (tel. 117-6222).
Opera: On the street next to the Opera House (tel. 132-8586). Good. Very appropriate for a meal before or after a performance.

Popular restaurants

There are many such restaurants in the city. During your trip, you will discover excellent popular restaurants serving the local residents as well as tourists. Here is a short and random list:

Halászkert: 46 Lajos utca. A cheerful restaurant in Obuda, specializing in fish dishes. Warm student atmosphere, with Gypsy music.
Hídvendéglö: 22 Mókus utca (tel. 188-6938). Quiet family restaurant, open only in the evenings.
Pest-Buda: 3 Fortuna utca (tel. 156-9849). Inexpensive restaurant on Castle Hill.
Alföldi: Keczkeméti utca, next to Kalvin tér, in Pest. Patronized especially by students and young Hungarians.
Paprika Csárda: 13 Bláthy Ottó utca, in Nefliget neighborhood (tel. 133-5972).

Ethnic restaurants

If you are tired of the heavy Hungarian food, you can find variety in fast-food restaurants (like *MacDonald's*) or in the different ethnic restaurants in the city.

Japan: 4 Luther utca (tel. 114-3427). An expensive Japanese restaurant whose decor is more interesting than its food.
Szecsuán: 5 Roosevelt tér (tel. 117-2502). Chinese. Less expensive, but the food is a pale version of the original.
Gőrőg Taverna: 24 Esengery utca (tel. 141-0772). Unpretentious restaurant with tasty food, resembling the taste of Greek food.
Napoletana: 3 Petőfi tér (tel. 118-5714), next to the *IBUSZ* office. Simple Italian food.

A number of other hotels and restaurants serve ethnic food. Full details are available in the restaurant guide in the booklet called "*Programme in Hungary*," published monthly and distributed to tourists in hotels and tourist bureaus.

Patisseries and cafés (cukrászda, kávehház)

In keeping with Hungary's past as part of the Austro-Hungarian Empire, the cáfes in Budapest serve excellent coffee and fine cakes.

Gerbeaud: 7 Vörösmarty tér, in the center of Pest. Also called Cafe Vörösmarty after the square where it is located. It has become a national institution since it opened in 1870. It is named after the Swiss baker Emule Gerbeaud, who bought the place in 1884 and, among other things, invented the cognac cake (*Konyakos Megy*), which is still sold here.
Ruszwurm: 7 Szentháromság utca, the equivalent of Gerbeaud in Buda, located on Castle Hill opposite Matthias Church. It opened in 1824, even supplying cakes to wealthy customers in Vienna who sent their servants to collect them. It is very tiny, and you may have to wait awhile for an empty table.
Café Quint: 1 Barczi István utca. Near the office of *Tourimform*, it is very pleasant and quiet, and retains the atmosphere of the city between the two world wars. Tasty cakes and excellent coffee. Closed on weekends.
Különlegességi: 70 Andrássy ut. Worth visiting.
Müvesz: 29 Andrássy utca. Near the Opera House. During the evening hours it is full of music lovers on their way to or from the opera.

Buda

Gellért Hill (Gellért hegy)

This hill, which rises above the city to a height of 140 meters, stands out day and night because of the impressive Liberation Monument at the top. It is a wonderful observation point and a good place to begin a tour of the city.

The hill is named after the bishop who spread Christianity throughout Hungary by order of the first Hungarian king, István. Legend has it that the honorable bishop was captured by the pagans who did not want to give up their faith and therefore put him into a barrel which they rolled from the summit of the hill down into the Danube River. Since then, the hill carries the bishop's name. On the slope of the hill which faces the Danube, we see the figure of Gellért waving his cross at the inhabitants of the city, surrounded by a circle of decorative pillars. The monument was constructed at the beginning of the century by the sculptor Jankovics.

On the hill is the **Citadel** (Citadella), a low fortress, built by the Austrian Hapsburg rulers in order to strengthen their hold over the inhabitants of the city after the Hungarian War of Independence (1848-1849). The fortress itself is not particularly interesting and has a hotel and restaurant. On the south side is the impressive **Liberation Monument** (Szabadság szobor) — a figure of a woman in the wind, rising to a height of 30 meters. The monument was built to be seen from all corners of the city. Ironically, historians point out, the monument was planned by Admiral Horthy and was built in 1947 by the Soviets — to commemorate the soldiers who fell in the battle for the liberation of the city from the Nazi occupiers.

It is possible to reach the summit of the hill by taxi or by bus No. 27 from the square in front of the entrance to the Citadella. Those so inclined can climb to the summit on foot via a lovely path which begins opposite Szabadság Bridge (about a 20 minute walk). If you have not managed to get to Gellért Hill during your visit to Budapest, go up to the summit on the last night of your stay in the city: the panorama of colored lights, the illuminated palaces, the bridges, and the river will remain engraved in your memory for a long time after you return home.

From Gellért Hill to Castle Hill

South of Gellért Hill stands the luxurious **Hotel Gellért**. Even if you do not intend to stay at the hotel, it is worth a visit, in order to enjoy its entertainment facilities and its thermal baths.

From the hotel we continue north along the Danube at the foot of Gellért Hill until **Rudas Bath-house** (Rudas fürdő), which was built by the Turkish pasha Mustafa Sokullu in 1566 and has retained its character and its beauty ever since, in particular, the rays of sunlight that are reflected through the colored glass.

After bathing, we continue north beside Elizabeth Bridge (Erszébet híd) on Attila utca to Szarvas tér. There we find the **Rac Bath-house** (Rácfürdő) (8-10 Hadnagy utca)

From Erzsébet Bridge to Gellért Hill

Bishop Gellért statue

located in a Turkish building from the 16th century, and the **Museum of the History of Medicine** (Semmelweis Orvostörténeti Múzeum, 1-3 Arpop utca; open Tues.-Sun. from 10:30am-6pm). In this house the Jewish doctor Fülöp Ignác Semmelweis lived and died (1818-1865). He discovered the connection between the death of infants and the lack of personal hygiene of doctors and nurses in the obstetrics department. His colleagues claimed that Semmelweis was insane and that such a link existed only in his imagination. Semmelweis remained adamant, and to prove his theory, he forced all the nurses and doctors in his department to wash their bodies and their hands and especially to sterilize their instruments. Since then, many mothers owe their lives and the lives of their infants to this doctor, who unfortunately went insane after his discovery was recognized. Nevertheless, he was accorded much renown, and his home has become a museum honoring him. From the Semmelweis Museum, Arpád utca leads to Lánchíd Street where we find another Turkish relic — the **market** (Várhegy Bazár) at the foot of Castle Hill, where fruit and vegetables were sold in the 17th century during the Turkish rule in the city. Lánchíd Street leads to **Adam Clark Square** (Clark Adam tér), named after the builder of the suspension bridge Széchenyi Lánchíd, constructed in the 19th century. It was the first permanent bridge in the city. Adam Clark Square is "point zero": from here the distances to other European cities are measured, and in the center of the square stands a stone statue which denotes this fact. From the square we go up to Castle Hill.

Castle Hill (Vár hegy)

Castle Hill is in the center of Buda. It is possible to reach this narrow elongated summit on foot from the suspension bridge (Széchenyi Lánchíd) by taxi or by bus No. 16, but most tourists prefer the special cable car (*Budavári Sikló*) which operates every day from 7:30am-10pm and connects Adam Clark Square with the palace on Castle Hill.

The story of the hill and the royal palace built on it is a microcosm of the history of Hungary itself. Settlement on the hill began in the middle of the 13th century, when King Béla IV built a fortress there to protect the region after the Mongol invasion. Sigismund of the House of Luxembourg built the first palace here at the beginning of the 15th century, in Gothic style, and King Matthias Corvinus expanded it in the second half of the 15th century. With the Turkish conquest, in 1541, the Hungarian king was banished, and the churches were used as mosques for the next 150 years, until Hungary was reconquered by Christians led by Hapsburg Austria (1686). During the period of the Austro-Hungarian Empire, the fortress on the hill developed; streets, houses, and many public buildings were constructed. Even though the rulers lived in Vienna and not in Buda, the palace continued to expand and develop.

After the First World War and the fall of the Empire, Admiral Horthy, who ruled with the support of the Nazis, occupied the palace, until they drove him out in 1944. During 1944-1945 it was under prolonged Russian siege. In the course of the battle, the palace and most of the old buildings were completely destroyed, but restoration work began in the early 1950's and the palace was reconstructed.

Today, the reconstructed **Royal Palace**, located in the southern part of the hill, houses museums. The most prominent is the **National Gallery** (Nemzeti Galeria) in the central and western wings.

The museum, which presents the history of Hungarian art, is open Tues.-Sun. from 10am-6pm.

In the room to the left of the entrance are stone sculptures, including remains from the Roman period until the Middle Ages and the Renaissance period. A special gallery on the second floor is devoted to Gothic altars brought here from different churches throughout Hungary. In other galleries we find altars from later periods.

On the second floor, 19th century art is displayed. The most outstanding artists here are Bertalan Székely, Gyula Benczúr, and Mihály Munkacsy, who has been honored with a gallery especially dedicated to him.

A place of honor is set aside for the artist Tivadar Csontváry Kosztka (see also the section on Pécs about the museum dedicated to him), some of whose paintings are exhibited on the half-level between the second and top floors. These include a painting of Jerusalem from 1905, encircled by a background of blue sea...

The top floor of the museum is devoted to 20th century art. Visitors to this floor can clearly see the modern construction in the postwar renovation of the Royal Palace.

In the southern wing of the Royal Palace is the **Budapest Museum of History** (Budapesti Történeti Múzeum). The exhibit begins on the ground floor, where there are neolithic remains from the fourth millenium BC, continuing chronologically on the first floor. The exhibition includes such historical remains as road signs, the first printing press in the city, and items from everyday life such as home furnishings and clothing. It covers the development of the city until the Soviet occupation in 1945, in a colourful and interesting display.

From the museums, continue north via Disz Square (Disz tér; from there busses leave for Moscow Square at the foot of the fortress), and on Tárnok utca until you reach Holy Trinity Square (Szentháromság tér), where the beautiful Matthias Church is located.

Matthias Church (Mátyás Templom) was built in the 15th century. It was erected on the ruins of an earlier church, apparently the first on Castle Hill, which was built in the 13th century. Here, in Matthias Church, King Charles Robert of the Anjou Dynasty was crowned after the official ceremony in Székesfehérvár. The church assumed its present form, both inside and out, when it was renovated at the end of the 19th century in neo-Gothic style. Its name came from the fact that it was the scene of the wedding of King Matthias and Queen Beatrix.

The church nave is awesome in its majesty. The glorious colored stained glass windows from the 19th century describe events from the lives of Christian figures. To the right of the apse, stairs lead to the church museum, whose corridors are more interesting than what is exhibited in the museum (remains from the tombs of Hungarian kings in Székesfehérvár).

After the church was completed in the 19th century, it was decided to beautify it, and on the side of the hill facing Pest, an ornate fortress called **Fishermen's Bastion** (Halászbástya) was built, at the top of a luxurious staircase. The name comes from a local tradition according to which members of the fishermen's guild would defend this side of Castle Hill during the battles of the Middle Ages. In fact, the fortress is no more than an ornament but is very impressive indeed, affording a wealth of possiblilties for photos from exciting angles.

North of Matthias Church is the local **Hilton Hotel**. This luxury hotel is located on an archeological site which was discovered while digging the foundations of the hotel. These

BUDAPEST — CITY CENTER

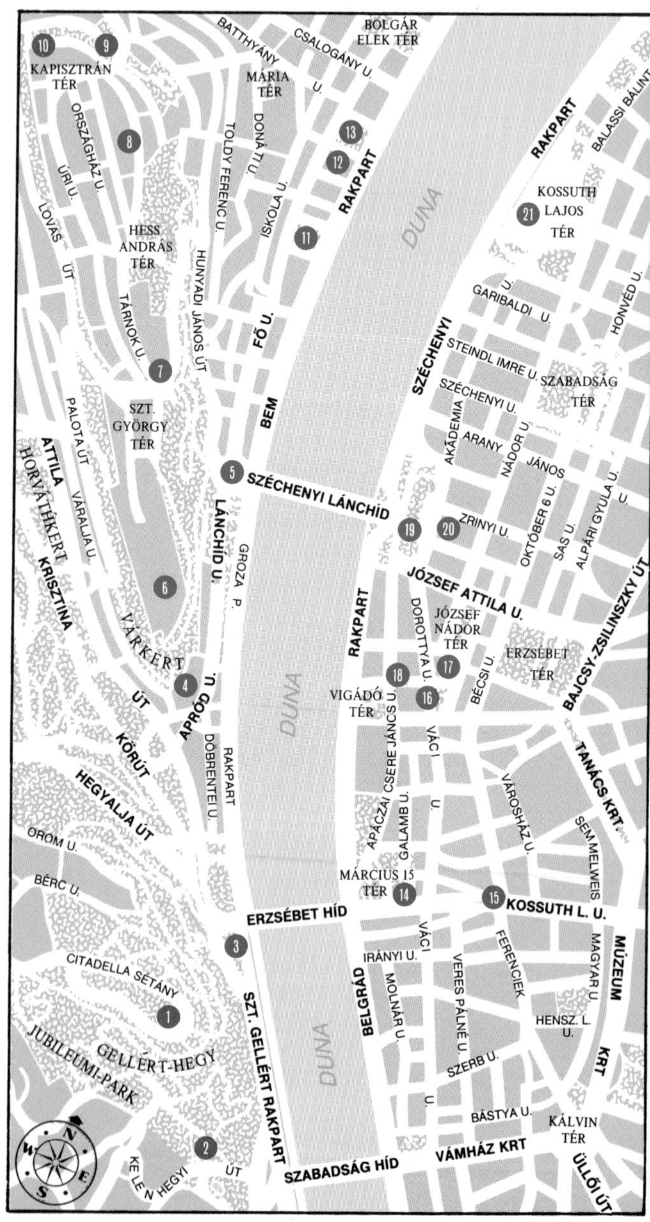

HUNGARY

Castle Hill

Index

1. Citadel
2. Gellért Hotel
3. Rudas Bath-House
4. Semmelweis Museum
5. Adam Clark Square
6. Royal Palace
7. Matthias Church
8. Old Synagogue
9. Vienna Gate
10. Museum of Military History
11. Calvinist Church
12. St. Anne's Church
13. Batthyány Square
14. City Parish Church
15. Felszabadulás Square
16. Vörösmarty Square
17. Gerbeaud Cafe
18. Vigadó
19. Roosevelt Square
20. Gresham Palace
21. Parliament

remains were not removed but rather were integrated into the construction of the building. They are an attraction even for tourists who are not staying in the hotel or gambling at its casino.

Táncsics Mihály utca leads north from the *Hilton*, bringing us to Erődy Palace (house No. 7), in which Beethoven lived during his visit to the city. The house at No. 9 is built on the ruins of the building which served as the royal residence prior to the construction of the luxurious palace on the southern part of the hill. This area was the Jewish Quarter in the 14th-16th centuries. It had two synagogues, one of which remains at No. 26 on this street.

The synagogue is open during the tourist season (May-October), Tues.-Fri. from 10am-2pm, and on weekends from 10am-6pm.

At the end of the street stands **Vienna Gate** (Bécsi Kapu), one of the important gates of the fortress, which was built during the 16th century, destroyed in the 19th century, and rebuilt in 1936 to mark 250 years since the liberation from the Turkish conquest. From Vienna Gate go down Castle Hill to the north or continue walking through the picturesque streets.

From Kapisztrám Square beside Vienna Gate, turn toward Tóth Arpád sétány, to visit the **Museum of Military History** (Hadtörténeti Múzeum) at No. 40. By using models, weapons, maps, documents, and battle plans, the museum surveys the military history of Hungary from the time of the Magyar conquest (at the end of the 9th century), through the wars of the Middle Ages, the 1848 revolution, and the wars of the 20th century. The second floor is devoted entirely to the First and Second World Wars. Open Tues.-Sun. 10am-6pm.

After a visit to the museum, one can wander through the lovely streets and relax in one of the restaurants (*Aranyhordo*, 16 Tárnok utca; open all week 10am-12 midnight) or the famous coffee-house *Ruszwurm* (7 Szentháromság utca), opposite Matthias Church (closed Wednesdays).

If you have time to spare, explore the network of underground caves on Castle Hill which have been dug out of the limestone rock of the hill. These caves and cellars were used in the Middle Ages to store food and wine. In the course of time, many tunnels and passages were dug which, later, served the needs of the army and as hideouts for people during the Second World War. A small section of the caves has been reconstructed and opened to the public as a small wax museum (the entrance is from 9 Uri utca; open Tues.-Sun. from 10am-6pm).

From the Castle Hill, we return to Adam Clark tér and continue our walk in the Viziváros area (City of Water) where there are many churches. Fő utca leads north from the Square to Szilágyi Dezső tér. In this square is the **Calvinist Church** (Kálvinista Templom), built with red bricks, at the end of the 19th century in a neo-Gothic style.

A bit north of this beautiful church along Fő utca is **St. Anne's Church** (Szent Anna Templom), built in the middle of the 18th century and considered the most beautiful Baroque church in the city. It is located in Batthyány Square. On the other side of this square is another impressive church, the Church of the Sisters of St. Elizabeth (Erzsébet Apácák Templom), built in 1737 on the ruins of a Turkish mosque. It has a monastery and a hospital.

Continuing along Fő utca, we come to the interesting **king's bath-house** (Király fürdő) at house No. 84. It was built by the Turkish Pasha Sokullu in 1570. It has a large pool and steam rooms under the rounded dome (see the section "bath-houses" in this chapter).

We turn left in Bem József utca toward bustling **Moscow Square** (Moszkva tér) or continue from this street north on Mártirok utca to visit the Franciscan Church of Buda at No. 23 and the grave of the Turkish saint **Gül Baba** (Gül Baba türbéje) at 14 Mecset utca. The grave may be visited during the tourist season Tues.-Sun. from 10am-6pm.

Frankel Leó utca leads us north to Óbuda, the old part of Buda, and to the continuation of our walk.

Óbuda

North of Buda is its old part — Óbuda. The first organized settlement here was a camp of the Roman Legions in 90 AD. There were 25,000 soldiers and servants living in the camp, and it soon became the capital of the Roman province of Lower Pannonia. The civilian Roman city built alongside the military camp was called Aquincum.

The merchants, craftsmen, clergymen, and others who lived in Aquincum earned their livelihood by working for the legionnaires. Baths-houses, streets, ancient homes, and more have been uncovered here.

Matthias Church

The most significant ruins which have been uncovered are those of the **Roman Amphitheater** (Katonai Tábor Amfiteátrum) near the intersection of Nagyszombati and Bécsi Streets. The amphitheater was built in the middle of the 2nd century AD and could seat about 12,000 spectators. A fortress was built on its remanents; the builders made use of the walls and stones remaining from the àmphitheater.

The **Roman Camp Museum** (Római Tábor Múzeum) at 63 Korvin Ottó utca is open during the tourist season Tues.-Sun. from 10am-6pm. It is located in a restored Roman house from the 3rd century AD.

Apart from these attractions, there are some other ruins from the Roman period. A **military bath-house** (Katonai Város Kozfürdóje), was erected for the Roman Legionnaires

The Fishermen's Bastion — a fortress for decoration only

(open during the tourist season Tues.-Sun. from 10am-6pm; found at 3 Flórián tér). There is also a large residential building, **Hercules Villa**, whose lovely mosaic floors depict that mythological hero. The site is located at 21 Meggyfa utca, and it can be visited during the tourist season on weekdays 10am-2pm and on weekends 10am-6pm.

In the center of Óbuda, east of Flórián tér is **Zichy Kastély** (1 Fő tér), a lovely palace in Baroque style built in 1757 and used today as a cultural center. Next to the palace you can visit **Verge Imre museum** (7 Laktanya utca). At the famous Hungarian sculptor's home are exhibited works which attract art lovers from around the world (open Tues.-Sun. from 10am-6pm).

From Flórián tér continue up Szentendrei utca, to reach another site at house No. 139, completing our tour of this side of the Danube. This is a site from the ancient city of **Aquincum** (Polgár-Város Pomterűcet). This archeological site contains the remains of streets, buildings, and shops — not especially impressive, and the visitor will need to use his imagination in order to visualize what it must have been like. Open during the tourist season Tues.-Sun. from 10am-5pm.

From here return to the center of town by taxi, bus, or the *HEV* suburban train to Batthyány tér, where there is a subway station which can take you anywhere in the city.

The Danube — bridges and islands

The bridges which connect Buda to Pest contribute much to the city's landscape. Construction of the permanent bridges began in the middle of the last century, but during World War II, they were all destroyed. In the winter of 1944-1945, people say, the ice on the river turned red with the blood of the casualties from the bitter battles. After the war, the bridges were rebuilt.

The most northerly bridge is **Arpád Bridge** (Arpád híd), which connects Károly Boulevard (Robert Károly Körút) in Pest with Margit Island and with Obuda. The bridge was opened to traffic in 1950. This is the best way to reach Margit Island by car.

Margit Bridge (Margit híd), 637 meters long, was built in 1876 in order to connect István Boulevard (Szt. István Körút) in Pest with Buda. An extension of the bridge reaches the southern end of Margit Island.

The **Széchenyi Suspension Bridge** (Széchenyi Lánchíd) is the most impressive bridge in the city. It is 350 meters long and was the first permanent bridge built to connect Buda and Pest. The bridge leads from the inner city in Pest (Belváros) to Adam Clark Square, at the foot of Castle Hill in Buda.

The bridge was planned in 1839 by the engineer William Clark, and the construction, which took until 1849, was supervised by Adam Clark (even though they have the same surname, they were not related). The bridge is embellished with fine statues of lions.

Elizabeth Bridge (Erszébet híd), 290 meters long, was built during the 1960's to replace the suspension bridge which had been built at the beginning of the century and was destroyed during the Second World War. The bridge leads from the center of Pest to the foot of Gellért Hill and the Citadel.

Liberty Bridge (Szabadság híd) which was also rebuilt in 1946, after the Second World War, to replace a bridge built at the end of the 19th century. It is 331 meters in length. The bridge is decorated with the legendary eagle-like bird, the *Turul*, which was the emblem of early Hungarians. The bridge connects Vámház körut in Pest with southern Buda.

The original **Petőfi Bridge** (Petőfi híd) was completed on the eve of the Second World War and was rebuilt in 1952. It connects Ferenc Boulevard (Ferenc körút) with southern Buda.

Margit Island (Margitsziget) is located between Arpád Bridge and Margit Bridge. The island, referred to in former times as "Rabbit Island", bears the name of Princess Margaret, the daughter of King Béla IV. Legend has it that the king swore that he would give his daughter to the church if he defeated the invading Mongols. Indeed, after his victory, the princess, aged 9, did enter the convent which was built on the island, where she lived until her death (1271).

Later, the island became an entertainment and vacation center for the Hungarian aristocracy, and hotels, palaces, and parks were built there, especially during the reign of the Hapsburgs. Today, it is the most beautiful park in the city, and visitors can wander through it in bicycle carriages, available for hire by tourists. Remains of the monastery and the churches on the island are not especially interesting, but it is worth walking taking a walk in the area, especially with children. Here, they will find a spacious playground with warm fish ponds and flower gardens, while the adults can wait for them in the open, shaded cafes beside the large hotels.

Széchenyi bridge

On Margit Island

Pest

Pest, located on the plain at the bend in the river, east of Buda, is the center for the business, shopping, and social life of the Hungarian capital. Originally, it was a fortress, built as a position in the first line of defense during the Roman period, then called Contra-Aquincum. At the site of the Roman fortress, an inner city developed (*Belváros*). In the 19th century a middle belt was built around the inner city, bordered by the great boulevards (*Nagy körút*), Szt. István, József, and Ferenc Boulevards, and the Margit Bridge over the Danube in the north and the Petőfi in the south. Except for a few sites, the other parts of Pest are less interesting and are made up mostly of residential areas and huge housing projects fitting the usual socialist formula.

Belváros

Elizabeth Bridge (Erzsébet híd) leads from Buda to Március 15 tér (March 15th Square) in the center of the inner city. The name commemorates the day when the War of Independence broke out in 1848. In one of its corners one can still find the ruins of the Roman city which was located here in the 2nd and 3rd centuries AD.

The **City Parish Church** (Belvárosi Templom), which stands in the square was built originally as a chapel, with stones from the Roman fortress, in the 12th century. It was destroyed during the Mongol invasion in the 13th century, rebuilt and expanded in Gothic style in the 15th century, and served as a mosque during the Turkish regime in the 18th century.

The church is not particularly beautiful, but history and architecture enthusiasts will enjoy visiting it and seeing the influence of the changing times and styles on the church. The prayer recess pointing to Mecca from the days of the Turkish mosque still exists, along with wall paintings from the 15th century, Gothic seating recesses (Sedilia), marble decorations in Renaissance style from the 16th century, and Baroque prayer altars — the multitude of styles reflecting the changes which occurred in the life of the city.

Continue a bit on Szabad sajtó utca, eastward. Cross the famous Vaci utca (we will come back to it later for entertainment and shopping) and you will arrive at Felszabadulás tér, center of the old city. This lovely square evolved from a small street (150 years ago) into a bustling business center, with many impressive buildings. Among them are the Savings Bank (Takarékpénztár), built in 1911 and also the residential apartments of Princess Klotild (Klotild Paloták), built in 1902 in the grand Baroque style.

Also in the square is the **Franciscan Church** (Ferencz Templom), built in the Baroque style in the first half of the 18th century on the ruins of a Turkish mosque. In front of the church is a lovely fountain (Nereidák Kútja), built in 1835 in the Classical style.

From the square we can return via Kigyó utca to the famous **Vaci utca** shopping mall, inundated with acrobats, street musicians and vendors. You can take a pleasant walk among the shops on both sides of the street which offer Hungarian folklore items, ranging from embroidered blouses to colored eggs, as well as fashionable modern clothing (unlike the somewhat outmoded styles common in Eastern Europe), excellent delicatessens, book stores, record shops, etc.

Váci utca takes you to bustling **Vörösmarty tér**. Clowns, street musicians, and portrait painters await the tourists here. Especially famous here is the *Cafe Gerbeaud* on the north side of the square. After sitting in the cafe and resting from the tour and the shopping, you may wish to head for the nearby *Philharmonia* ticket office (1 Vörösmarty tér), to purchase tickets for the concerts or opera performances which take place in the city.

From Belváros to the Parliament

Our tour along the bank of the Danube begins at the **City Parish Church** (already mentioned in the previous tour), from which we go north to Petöfi tér. At this square stands the **Greek-Orthodox Church** (Ortodox Templom), built in the Baroque style at the end of the 18th century for the community of Greek merchants in the city (open during the tourist season from 10am-5pm).

From Petöfi tér, we continue along the delightful promenade on the river bank. Beyond the luxury hotel *Duna Intercontinental* is Vigadó tér, where the concert hall of Pest is located in magnificent **Vigadó Palace**. The palace was built in the middle of the 19th century and is an outstanding example of the Hungarian Romantic style which developed in the city. The auditorium was opened to the public in 1865 with a world premiere of Liszt's composition, *St. Elizabeth*.

From Vigadó Palace, we continue alongside the quay, past

the *Forum* and *Atrium Hyatt* hotels to Roosevelt Square at the edge of the impressive Széchenyi Bridge. Opposite the bridge is **Gresham Palace** (Gresham Palota), built in art nouveau style at the beginning of the century for an English insurance company. Alongside it is the **Hungarian Academy of Sciences** (Magyar Tudományos Akadémia). Entrance to the Academy is forbidden, but this magnificent neo-Renaissance building can be viewed and enjoyed from the outside. It was built in 1864 on the initiative of Count Széchenyi, who played a significant role in promoting the building up of the city in the first half of the 19th century. From the Academy of Sciences, Akadémia Street (Akadémia utca) leads to the Parliament building.

The **Parliament** (Országház) is one of the most prominent buildings in the city. It has 691 rooms and immense halls. The Parliament was built in a neo-Gothic style by the architect Steindl Imre. He began his work in 1885, age 46, and died in 1902, only a few months before it was opened, when the building had already been under construction for 17 years. From any angle, the building is impressive, but the most photographed side is the one which faces the Danube. On the other side of the building is a broad green square, where national ceremonies are held on occasion. The eclecticism of Steindl is prominent in his work. The facade of 268 meters, whose towers overlook the Danube, rises to the height of 72 meters (the dome reaches 96 meters), presenting simultaneously such a variety of styles that it is sometimes difficult to isolate its elements.

The grandeur and elegance of the building have brought much criticism upon it, such as the Hungarian poet who facetiously argued that the building is nothing more than a Turkish bath in a Gothic church. Still, a visit to this grand, perhaps overly ostentatious building is a must.

You can only visit the Parliament building with an organized group on Monday, Wednesday, and Friday at 10:30am between May and October. You can join (via the *IBUSZ* office) such a tour, which leaves the *IBUSZ* platform in the bus station in Erzsébet tér (it includes a visit to Castle Hill). It is also possible to arrange a group at short notice or to join an organized tour (free, but there may not be a place). Entrance to the palace is from gate 12 on Mondays and Fridays at 10am, 11am, and 2pm (additional details and reservations at tel. 112-3500, ext.437).

Opposite the Parliament building, on the other side of the

The center of Pest

square, is the **Ethnographic Museum** (Néprajzi Múzeum) at 12 Kossuth Lajos tér. This interesting museum is located in a palace which was originally built for the supreme court at the end of the 19th century. At the top of the building is a statue of the blind goddess of justice. The large decorated hall which we see upon entering the museum (open Tues.-Sun. from 10am-6pm) gives an idea of the building's beauty. There are exhibitions which describe different ways of life, beginning with pre-historic times and including Eskimo villages and replicas of African rites.

We complete our tour along the Danube in the nearby *Cafe Szalai*, which remained in private hands even after the nationalization of Hungary in 1956 (7 Balassi Bálint utca, north of the Parliament).

The Parliament

The Kis körút — From the National Museum to the great Basilica

We begin our walk through the boulevards which surround the inner city at Kálvin tér, the former location of a gate to the inner fortified city. In the northern part of the square is the **National Museum** (Nemzeti Múzeum) at 14-16 Múzeum körút. The museum, which is the largest in the country, was built in the years 1836-1846 by Mihály Pollák and is a beautiful example of the city's neo-Classical architecture. At the entrance you can buy a booklet describing the current exhibitions. Unfortunately, as in all other Hungarian museums, here, too, all the information is given only in Hungarian, what makes for great difficulty in finding your way among the diferent exhibitions and in understanding them.

The ground floor is devoted to archeological remains from before the the pre-Magyar period. The first floor is devoted to the period between the Magyar conquest and the War of Independence in 1848-1849. This exhibit is the focus of interest for tourists because of the royal crown from the 11th century and the royal jewels from the 15th-18th centuries displayed here. Also on show are the museum's collections of portraits, paintings, and Hungarian coins, as well as various temporary exhibits. On the top floor is an extensive and comprehensive exhibition of nature in Hungary — geology, flora, and fauna. (The museum is open Tues.-Sun. from 10am-6pm).

From the museum continue north on Múzeum körút (or continue through the underground passage) and cross Rákóczi utca to Tanács körút to visit the Jewish Quarter, where 230,000 Jews lived before the Second World War. The most impressive site in the quarter is the **Great Synagogue** (Szinagóga, 2-8 Dohány utca). This was the second largest synagogue in the world when it was built in the Romantic style between 1854-1859, with place for about 3,000 worshippers. From time to time, festive prayers are still held in it.

At the entrance to the **Jewish Museum** (Zsidó Múzeum) next door is a memorial tablet which explains that this is the birthplace of the Jew Herzl Tivádar (Theodore Herzl), the man who played a central role in founding the Zionist movement. The museum abounds in stirring artifacts from Jewish life in the Hungarian capital and gives some idea of the past glory of the community. At one end of the museum is a memorial room depicting the suffering of Hungarian Jewry in the Holocaust.

The synagogue and the museum are surrounded by Jewish graves and a memorial monument, commemorating Hungarian Jews who died during the First World War and those who were murdered by the Nazis during the Second World War. (Open during the tourist season Sun.-Fri. from 10am-1pm, and on Mon. and Thurs. also from 2-6pm.)

From the Jewish Quarter, Tanács Boulevard continues to Deák tér. Here we find the **Lutheran Church** (Deák Téri Evangelikus Templom), built at the beginning of the 19th century in neo-Classical style by the architect Pollack, who also built the National Museum. Here we also find the central subway station, where the three urban lines converge.

From this square we turn up Alpári Gyula utca to the **Great Basilica** (Szent István Bazilika), the largest church in Budapest. Construction of the church began in 1851, and a series of disruptions during its building (the death of the architect Hild in 1867, the collapse of the dome in 1868, the death of the architect Ybl in 1891) delayed its completion until 1905. The change of architects and of architectural styles during the course of the construction influenced its appearance. Its size is more impressive than its beauty.

A more beautiful building is the **Opera House** (Operaház) behind the Basilica (see the next tour). The building is located on Andrássy utja, one of the most attractive streets in the city. A pleasant walk along this street leads you to the city park.

Along Andrássy Boulevard

Andrássy Boulevard (Andrássy utja) is one of the loveliest and most impressive thoroughfares in Hungary's capital, and it is pleasant to walk along its 2.5 kilometer length. Work began during the building spurt in the 19th century. Take your time while walking along this wide boulevard, as almost every house and building here is worthy of your attention.

We begin our tour in Deák tér, where all three urban subway lines converge. After passing the large cathedral, we find on the right, at No. 25, the **Ballet School** (Allami Balettintézet), built during the 1880's in Renaissance style. On the left, at No. 22, is one of the most beautiful buildings in the entire city, the **Grand Opera House** (Magyar Allami Operaház).

After the land for the proposed Opera House was purchased,

The synagogue in Dohány street

The Hungarian Opera House

a competition was conducted among the architects. The winner was Ybl Miklós who submitted a plan for an elegant neo-Classical building. Construction lasted for nine years, and the opening ceremony took place on September 27, 1884. It immediately became an important center of culture. Gustav Mahler and other renowned composers worked here. During a daytime visit, the structure seems most impressive, and an evening at the opera completes the enjoyment of this neo-Classical auditorium.

Continuing along the boulevard, we reach Franz Liszt Square (Liszt Ferenc tér), where the **Academy of Music** (Liszt Ferenc Zeneművészeti Főiskola) is located. It was built in the art nouveau style during the first years of the 20th century. Every evening different classical concerts take place in the central auditorium here.

We pass Octogon tér, so callad because of its shape. From now on, the appearance of Andrássy Boulevard changes and it becomes wider and more spacious. At No. 69 is the puppet theater (Bábszinház), and at No. 71 is the **Academy of Fine Arts** (Magyar Képzőmüvészeti Főiskola), built in 1876 in the neo-Renaissance style. Two quite interesting museums are further up the street: the **Hopp Ferenc Museum of East-Asian Art** (at No. 103) with a fine collection from Indian culture, and the **Chinese Museum** (Kina Múzeum), which is part of the Hopp Ferenc Museum of East-Asian Art, at 12 Gorkifasor Street nearby. These museums are open Tues.-Sun. from 10am-6pm.

At the end of the previous century, the final section of this long boulevard began to attract the local aristocracy. They built their homes here, and today, the area has become one of the most prestigious in the city. Many of its lovely buildings house foreign embassies.

Andrássy Boulevard ends at Heroes' Square (Hősök tére). In the square, at the entrance to the municipal park, is the **Millenium Memorial** commemorating the conquest of Hungary by the Magyars.

The municipal park

The **municipal park** (Városliget), the largest park in Budapest, is located in northeast Pest on land used for the royal hunt by Hungarian kings. At the entrance to the park from the direction of Andrássy utja is the **Millenium Memorial** (Millenniumi Emlékmű), whose construction began in 1896 to commemorate one thousand years since the arrival of the first Magyars (896).

In the center of this elegant memorial stands a white marble pillar, and at its head is the angel Gabriel. The angel was accorded this honor after appearing in a dream of Pope Sylvester II ordering him to send the royal crown to Hungary, thus showing support for its king in his efforts to establish the hold of Christianity in the country. Around the pillar are statues of the seven leaders of the Magyar tribes who conquered Hungary and made it their home. The two wings of the memorial continue to tell the story of the country by means of various sculptures and reliefs, which depict the country's leaders during the past thousand years.

On the northwest side of the Millenium Memorial is the **Museum of Fine Arts** (Szépművészeti Múzeum), containing the largest collection of art in the country. The impressive collection on exhibit in the museum includes the works of Raphael, Rembrandt, El Greco, Breughel, Renoir, and many more of the greatest painters in the world.

The most outstanding collection in the museum is on the first floor and includes works of the greatest painters of

Europe from the 13th to the 20th centuries. Room 5 shows the works of Titian, Tintoretto and others. In room 8 are the works of Raphael, and in rooms 9-11 the works of Breughel and Rembrandt stand out. The opposite wing is devoted to Spanish painters, the most well-known being El Greco (room 15) and Goya (room 17). The collection of French art further on is also impressive and includes the works of Renoir, Monet, Cezanne, and others.

In November 1983 in this museum, occurred one of the largest art thefts of the 20th century. Seven outstanding works, including two paintings of Raphael, were stolen with amazing ease, because of the poor security at the museum. Two months later, the paintings were found and the Italian thieves apprehended.

The museum is open Tues.-Sun, from 10am-6pm. The Spanish wing (*Spanyol szárny*) is open from 10am-1pm, and the Italian wing (*Olasz szárny*) is open from 2-6pm.

Behind this museum is the famous *Gundel* restaurant, considered one of the best in the city. Advance reservations are required (tel. 122-1002). Try this excellent and expensive restaurant. (open 12 noon-4pm and 7pm-12 midnight).

On the other side of the square is a building whose exterior is more impressive than its inside — the **Art Gallery** (Műcsarnok). The building was built in 1895 and, today, it houses temporary exhibits.

Beyond the Millenium Monument, we turn to the **Vajdahunyad Castle** on a small island in the middle of an artificial lake. In winter, most of the water is removed from the lake, and the rest serves ice-skating enthusiasts. The castle was built for the millenium exhibition at the end of the 19th century. Its purpose was to serve as a model showing and preserving the country's architecture. Following the success of the exhibition, the model was replaced by a permanent structure at the beginning of the 20th century. Today, the castle houses the Agriculture Museum, which depicts the development of agriculture in Hungary from the days of the Magyars until our times.

Children, as well as adults, can enjoy the wealth of amusement possibilities available in the large park. You can begin the walk with a visit to the **Zoo** and the **Botanical Garden** (Fővárosi Allatkert Es Növénykert). The zoo was built in the last century, and its 500 animals live in quite small cages. Farther on is the

Grand Circus (Fővárosi Nagycirkusz), which has several performances each day. Some of the best foreign circuses appear here, including the Moscow Circus (details at the *Tour Inform* agency and in the entertainment section of the English language daily paper, the *Daily News*).

In addition to the circus, there is an **amusement park** (Vidam Park) with many obsolete structures. The **Transport Museum** (Kőzlekedési Múzeum) in the municipal park is of no special interest.

The **Széchenyi Bath-house** in the park is the place to end your walk — with a bath in the warm pools to relax your tired muscles.

Buda Hills

Buda Hills are more than just another green park in the city. They are a huge amusement area, with scenic walking trails. A visit and a stay in this park are very highly recommended, after you have spent several days in the bustle of the city.

You can reach this site by car, tram, or by bus No. 56 which leaves from Moskva tér (at the foot of Castle Hill). But the most interesting way to travel to the park is on the picturesque *mountain train* (Fogaskerekű) which takes the visitor from the hotel area of the city to the top of **Szabadság hegy**. A **chair lift** (Libegó) leads from Zugliget (Liberty Hill) utca to the highest summit in the region, János hegy (529 meters high).

While visiting the hills, don't miss a ride on the Pioneer Railway run by children, members of the youth movement, under the supervision of railroad workers. The train leaves from Hüvos Völgy to Széchenyi Hill (Széchenyi hegy) via the lovely hilltops. In addition to these entertaining trips during the tourist season, another attraction is a stalactite and stalagmite cave (Pálvölgy Cseppköbarlang) south of Matthias Hill (Mátyás hegy) at 162 Szépvölgyi utca. The cave is partially lit for daytime visitors (during the tourist season). From the cave, continue on your nature walk to Hármashatár Hill (497 meters high). Near the summit is a camping site, pleasant restaurant, and a path to an observation lookout at the summit.

Bath-houses

One hundred and fifty years of Turkish rule in Hungary made bath-houses (fürdő) part of everyday life in Hungary. The

The Millenium Monument

abundance of warm springs found in the city and throughout the country enabled Hungarians to continue to enjoy this customs and to make it an integral part of their life-style. The springs were formed as a result of the movement of mountain ranges, causing geological rifts through which warm spring waters gushed.

A selection of Budapest bath-houses
Rudas: a pleasant Turkish bath with steam rooms and several pools of different temperatures at the foot of Gellért Hill. Open to men only — on weekdays from 6am-7pm and on weekends until 1pm. There is also a large pool for use by men and women together, but it is not very clean. The address: 9 Döbrentei tér.
Gellért: in Gellért Hotel there are separate hot baths for women and men as well as a mixed pool. The water contains minerals which are very beneficial for health. The baths and pool are very clean. Massages, pedicures, etc. are also available. Open daily from 7am-7pm. The address: 1 Gellért tér, south of Gellért Hill.
Rac: a Turkish bath from the 15th century. Rather dilapidated. Open on weekdays for women only. The address: 8-10 Hadnagy utca, between Gellért Hill and Castle Hill.
Kiraly: This pleasant bath was built in the 16th century, also by the Turks. The building is charming and interesting, but it is in need of basic renovation. Open for men and women on alternate days (Mon. Wed. Fri. for men and Tues. Thurs. Sat. for women). Closed on Sundays. The address: 84 Fő utca.
Thermal: in the *Thermal* luxury hotel (on Margit Island), opened in 1979, has hot pools and medicinal baths, fed by waters which are brought from the hot springs in the area. The pool is clean but lacks something of the old Turkish charm of the other bath-houses.
Széchenyi: the lovely bath-house in the municipal park is fed from hot springs whose waters flow at a temperature of 75 degrees Celsius. The water reaches the large pool at a temperature of 27 degrees Celsius. There are both open and covered pools. Relaxation in the pools and on the rolling lawns beside them can be an excellent conclusion to your visit in the city. Regrettably, the place is fairly noisy and very crowded. The address: 9 Allatakerti körút.

Sports

The multitude of sports events which take place in the Hungarian capital attract many spectators: for example, international soccer games, held in the large stadium, **Népstadion** near the Keleti railroad station, or the Hungarian League games, held in the local stadiums (more details in the daily English language newspaper, *Daily News*).

Gymnastic competitions on an international level and other types of sports events take place in the mammoth Sports Arena (Sportcsarnok), on the other side of the Keleti railroad station (more details in the magazine *Programme*).

Horse races are held at two main centers: one is for trotters (9-11 Kerepesi út), and the other for regular riding (10 Dobo István utca).

A marathon race is held in April, and a *Grand Prix* auto race is held in the summer.

For the children

The childrens' stay can be made enjoyable with a visit to the **pantomime** performances of the *Domino* troupe, which are suitable for adults as well and take place in the theater wing of the Vigadó Concert Hall. Another event for children is the **puppet theater**. Performances are held several times a day in the State Puppet Theater at 69 Andrássy utja (for details and ticket reservations, phone tel. 142-2702) and in the theater on Jókai tér (details and reservations at tel. 142-2622).

Children will also enjoy the wax museum in the caves of Castle Hill (entrance from 9 Uri utca) and the collection of reptiles and fish at the Aquarium/Terrarium (entrance from Párizsi utca in the center of Pest).

A Soviet space exhibition, which looks like a very small replica of the Space Museum in Washington is found in the **Planetarium** in the Nepliget Quarter. Here there are also impressive laser shows (Lézer-Multimédia Fénykoncert) to the accompaniment of contemporary music, like Pink Floyd, Mike Oldfield, Jean Michel Jarre, etc. The programs take place several times each evening (for details, call tel. 113-8280 and see the monthly brochure).

Bowling alleys can be found in the modern *Novotel* hotel, where both parents and children can bowl after a day of travel and entertainment.

The classics at Vigadó

Night life

Concerts, Opera, and Ballet

Concerts of classical music are held in Budapest nightly. A thin black booklet, *Koncert Kalendárium*, is distributed monthly in hotels and tourist agencies with details about concerts planned for the coming month. Additional information can be found in the monthly booklet *Programme in Hungary* and in the entertainment column of the local *Daily News*. Most concerts begin at 7:30pm.

The following are some of the main concert halls in Budapest:

Vigadó: 2 Vigadó tér, tel. 117-6222. Concerts held every evening; the large auditorium is especially luxurious.
Academy of Music (Zene Akademie): 8 Liszt Ferenc tér, tel.

142-0179. Concerts and recitals take place in the large hall.
State Opera House (Operáház): 22 Andrássy. Operas performed every evening. An impressive auditorium and balconies. Mostly performed in Hungarian translation.
Erkel Theater: 30 Köztársaság tér. The large hall appears drab from the outside; inside it is modern, with excellent acoustics. Opera and dance performances.

Tickets for the performances are available at the ticket booths of the halls themselves until curtain time, but it is advisable to purchase them in advance at the *Philharmonia* ticket office — 1 Vörösmarty tér (behind Vigadó Concert Hall).

Another centrally located ticket office can be found near the State Opera House, 18 Andrássy utja. Ticket prices are inexpensive.

Folkdancing and folklore performances
On weekends, some clubs (*Tanácz Ház*) in the city, especially in the suburbs, offer evenings of Hungarian folkdancing. Enthusiasts can join the circle of dancers or enjoy watching the professional dance troupes, which perform several times each month in the youth center in the municipal park (19 Zichy Mihály utca). Performances begin at 7pm. Exact details are available in the booklet *Programme*. Tickets are available at the performance.

Theater and musicals
Those who speak Hungarian will enjoy the plays presented nightly at the theaters in the capital. Language problems almost vanish in Hungarian versions of international musicals, such as *Cats* and *Evita*, with their wealth of colorful costumes and exciting dances, which try to imitate the successful western stage productions. Details can be found in the monthly booklet *Programme*.

Tickets are sold at the theater entrance (if any are left) or at tourist bureau offices. A central ticket agency is located at 18 Andrássy.

Night clubs
Tourist bureaus in the city offer a night tour which includes a visit to a folk club. In the club, a typical Hungarian meal is served to the tune of Gypsy music, and the participants are invited to join the traditional dancing. You can sign up for such a tour at *IBUSZ* offices.

In Budapest there are also lively night clubs, where magicians, comedians, and erotic dancers perform. The most prominent of these are:

Mayin: three performances every evening at 8pm, 11pm, and 1am. In the *Emke Hotel*, 3 Akácfa utca, tel. 122-7858.
Moulin Rouge: performances at 10pm, midnight, and 1:45am, at 17 Nagymező utca, tel. 112-4492.
Orfeum: the famous night club in Hotel Beke. Performances begin at 10:45pm and 1am (tel. 132-3300).

Casino

The casino of Budapest is located in the *Hilton Hotel* on Castle Hill. In the casino are roulette tables, blackjack, slot machines, etc. Bets are made with chips bought only with foreign currency. The casino is open from 5pm until the wee hours of the morning. There is an entrance fee of 5 German Marks, for which you receive chips in exchange.

Shopping

Famous Váci utca in the center of town is the traditional and prestigious shopping center, where you will find the widest range of merchandise in the country. On this street there are many shops, such as *Fontana* (clothing accessories, at No. 16), the excellent bookshop *Libri* (at No. 32), and the *Philantelia* flower shop (at No. 9) in a neo-Classical style building, which hints at the original form which the street had in the 19th century. You will enjoy walking along this enticing street and noting the variety of boutiques and shops which offer the tourist the latest in fashions, musical equipment and supplies, Hungarian and Russian delicacies, and folklore items (such as embroidered blouses). The latter are sold, among other places, at the *Intertourist* shop at No. 14.

Porcelain products of the world-famous *Herend* or *Zsolnai* companies can be purchased at the central *Intertourist* shop on Kigyo Street near Váci. The shop is not cheap, but it has a large collection of ceramic ware along with other folk items. Purchases are in foreign currency only.

Hungarians prefer to shop in the large department stores (*áruhaz*) in the city rather than in the expensive Váci shops. These department stores are overflowing with inexpensive merchandise, but the sales people are usually indifferent or uninterested and make one long for the smiling, multi-lingual Váci utca. The most prominent department stores include: *Corvin Aruház* in Blaha Aruhaz tér at the corner of Rákóczi utca and Erzsébet körut, and *Luxus Aruház*, at the corner of Rákóczi utca at 3 Vörösmarty tér.

The *Skála* chain has three large outlets: one at Marx Square (opposite the western railroad station), the second in Obuda (far away and not worth the effort to get there), and the third and largest, beside the *Gellért* hotel in Buda.

The best shops for foreign language books are located along Váci utca (including the excellent shop at No. 32), at 4 Kossuth Lajos utca and at No. 18 of the same street. At 4 Vörösmarty tér is another large shop. Among the wealth of books in English, German, and French, it is worth noting the colorful and inexpensive photography and art books of *Corvina*, the state publishing house.

Of the record shops, an outstanding one is located beside the *Philharmonia* ticket office (Vörösmarty tér).

The **fruit and vegetable market** (*Vásárcsarnok*) is open Mon.-Sat. during the day and closed on Sundays. It is not far from Szabadság Bridge. The colorful market, which is impressively large, offers exciting possibilities for photos, and is worth visiting.

The **Flea Market** (*Ecseri Piac*) is not at all colorful, but it has an impressive array of merchandise including old fashioned clothing which may one day come back into fashion. In this market there are plenty of bargains to be found by picking through the piles. In the center of the market, fashionable items are sold, such as jeans jackets and inexpensive leather coats, while all around are stalls and shops selling everything from antique porcelain pipes to screws, broken appliances, and old chests of drawers. The market is outside the city center, in the Kispest Quarter (56 Nagy Kőrösi). It is open Mon.-Sat. from 8am-3pm, but most of the activity takes place between 10am-2pm. On Sundays the market is closed. To get there, take a cab, since none of the busses or subway lines reach this point.

Special events

Undoubtedly, the main event in Budapest and in all of Hungary is the **Spring Festival**, which takes place during ten busy days at the end of March. Concerts and musical appearances of first-ranking Hungarian and international artists attract large audiences. Some of the concerts are held at interesting historical sites. The price of tickets to performances, as usual in Hungary, is not high, but they are

At the market

generally sold out long before the beginning of the festival.

The central office of the festival, where you can purchase tickets for performances, is located at 1 Vörösmarty tér; tickets may also be purchased at any *IBUSZ* office.

The Film Festival is the only festival which takes place in Budapest in winter. It is held at the beginning of February and lasts four days.

Liberation Day (April 4) is celebrated with parades and mass meetings. On Constitution Day, at the end of August, fireworks are sent skyward over the Danube. The music festival in the month of October closes the tourist season with local and imported musical events.

Important addresses in Budapest

Ambulance and Transport to Hospital: tel. 04.
Police: tel. 07.
Dental clinic (for emergencies): 52 Mária utca, tel. 133-0189.
Information about postal services and international information service in English: tel. 117-2200 (8am-2pm weekdays only).
IBUSZ information: tel. 117-9800 (24 hours a day).
Emergency service for cars: Magyar Autóklub, 4 Rómer lóris utca, tel. 135-3101.
Assistance in case of road accident: tel. 693-714, 691-831 (24 hours a day).
Train information: tel. 122-4052.
Interurban bus information: tel. 117-2562 (every day 6am-6pm).
Taxis: tel. 166-6666 (Volántaxi), tel. 122-2222 (*Főtaxi*). Flight information: Ferihegy 1 — tel. 157-2106.
Ferihegy 2 (for MALEV passengers) — tel. 157-7179.
Municipal hospital: Városi Körház, 69 Baross utca, tel. 169-0666.

Danube Bend (Dunakanyar)

The Danube, which is the second largest river in Europe, after the Volga, widens as it reaches the Carpathian Basin, changes its course from east to south, and forms the Danube Bend by making a sharp, almost right-angled turn. The combination of the broad silent river and the wooded hills creates a pastoral scene. The proximity of Danube Bend to Budapest allows for a lovely one-day outing, which can be made even by those who plan to visit only in Budapest.

The abundance of water and the wooded hills, which provide protection and shelter, have attracted inhabitants to this area, from pre-historic times until today. Now, it is a popular summer vacation spot, both for tourists and the local population. Over the years, the different population groups who settled here have left their mark on the Danube Bend by building beautiful cities with royal palaces, fortresses, impressive churches and more.

Most of the interesting historical sites are found on the western bank of the river. It is possible to take a one-day trip in the area which would include most of these sites. Your Budapest hotel can serve as both the starting point and final destination. Or else a more comprehensive visit could be planned for each site separately, including a stop-over at one of the hotels in the area.

How to get there

By boat To Esztergom: May 1 to September 3, direct ferries depart at 7:30am and 2pm, arriving five hours later. In April, there is one ferry only, at 7:30am, and in September and October, only at 2pm.
The Esztergom Ferry, which stops at Vác on the east bank and Visegrád, leaves at 6;45am. The trip lasts a little over five hours.

During the tourist season, a ferry leaves for **Visegrád** at 10am and arrives three hours later.

The return trip for all routes leaves about an hour after the boat arrives. During November-April, there is no ferry at all. On weekends and national holidays, there may be changes.

The main disadvantage of the boat trips is that they take a long time, so it is a good idea to sail in one direction (for example from

Budapest to Szentendre to Esztergom) and return to Budapest by bus or train.

More details about sailings are available at tel. 181-223.

By train: it is pleasant to go from Budapest to Pomáz and Szentendre by the suburban train (*HEV*) which leaves from Batthyány tér in Buda (opposite the Parliament) several times an hour. The 20 km trip takes only half an hour. Other trains leave for Vác on the eastern bank (2-3 times a day) from the western railroad station and to Esztergom (every hour) from the same station, a trip of about 80 minutes.

By bus: busses leave Erzsébet tér for Szentendre, Visegrád, and Esztergom at least once an hour. Those wanting to get to the Pilis hills can take a bus to Dobogókő which leaves once a day on weekdays and 3-4 times a day on weekends. Busses to Vác and the other towns on the east bank leave every hour from Bulcsú tér in Budapest.

By car: road 11 connects Budapest to sites on the western bank of the Danube. The distance from Budapest to Esztergom is 67 kms along the river and only 47 kms by road 10 coming from the south. The most beautiful route is via the road through the wooded Pilis hills, Pomáz, and Dobogókő. Road 2 and its continuation, road 12, are recommended for the trip from Budapest to the eastern bank, the bank of the Danube which is less frequented by tourists.

Szentendre

About 20 kms from Budapest lies the picturesque town of Szentendre, on the west bank of the Danube. It was first populated during the Stone Age, but the Romans were the first to build a permanent settlement here. The Roman city was called Ulcisia and was established in the 1st century AD, after the area was captured from the Illyrian tribes. It included a fortress enclosed by a wall and a small inner city which thrived until the arrival of the Huns in the 4th century.

Szentendre was rebuilt in the 12th century and renamed after St. András, the patron of the monastery located nearby. Serbian refugees who reached the vicinity during the 15th century, while fleeing from the Turkish conquerors, settled in the city. They were joined by more refugees from Balkan countries after the city was freed from the Turks in the 17th century. The influence of these refugees gave the city its unique and picturesque appearance: small homes and narrow streets which are very colorful and pleasing to the eye and to the taste of visitors. Today, 20,000 people live in the city, and it is famous for its many artists, museums, and galleries.

Szentendre

Danube Bend

In the village museum

Margit Kovács Museum

The **tourist information bureau** *Dunatours* is located at 6 Somogyi Bacspó (tel. 11-311), near the loading dock. The suburban train and the bus are a short walk away along Kossuth utca, south of the city center.

Food and lodging

If you decide to remain overnight in the city, you can stay at the dependable *Danubius* hotel (28 Adye utca, tel. 12-511); *Party* hotel, simpler and less expensive (same street No. 5, tel. 12-491); or at the *Domino* pension (No. 80, same street). Another unpretentious hotel, open during the tourist season, is the *Sziget* (tel. 10-697) on Szentendrei-Sziget Island in the Danube, opposite the city.

As to the city's restaurants, the *Vidám Szerzetesek Kisvendéglö* should not be missed (5 Vöröshadsereg utca, a bit north of Fő Square, tel. 363-240).

What to see

Fő tér, previously called Marx tér, is the central square in the city and the starting point for a tour of the town. In the square are the **Blagovestenska Eastern Orthodox Church** (Blagovestenska Templom), a Greek Serbian church, built in the Baroque style in 1752 and decorated with holy figures which are the work of Mikhail Zivkovic.

Hunyadi utca leads from the square northwest to the Serbian-Orthodox Church which is also called **Belgrade Church** (Belgrád Templom) and is surrounded by a pleasant garden. This church was built in the Baroque style (1756-1764) and the pictures of the saints in it were painted by the Serbian artist Vasilije Ostoic. Alongside the church is a **collection of holy artifacts** (Szerb Egyháztörténeti Gyujtemeny). If the church and the religious exhibit are closed, you can go to the house next door which is called Plebánia Csengője and ask them to let you in.

From the Serbian Church continue a few meters southward to Templom tér. Here, there is an enchanting view of the city rooftops and of the tranquil Danube. From the square, where pottery is sold on weekends, you can go down the stairs and return to Fő tér which is in the center of town.

Szentendre is famous for its many artists and especially for the ceramicist Margit Kovács, (1902-1977). An excellent museum of her works is located at 1 Vastagh György utca, next to the central square. It is not necessary to be an art or ceramics enthusiast to be impressed by the marvelous works of this artist. In the exhibit, open daily 9am-7pm, are many figures of women, performing everyday tasks. In the introduction to the booklet for visitors she writes: "Clay is the bread of my day, my joy and my sorrow. Since I first touched it, it has become the bedrock of my life and become a part of the life's blood circulating in my veins." There are many other museums and galleries in the city, including the museum of paintings and sculptures, opposite the entrance to the Margit Kovacs Museum. Art lovers can spend long hours going from one museum, gallery, and souvenir shop to another, since they are found in abundance in the center of the city.

The **Open-Air Village Museum** (Szabadtéri Néprajzi Múzeum), also called *Skansen* after the famous museum in Stockholm, is unique. Here, an attempt has been made to preserve ancient villages from different parts of Hungary. It is located about 3 kms west of the city along Szabadságforrás Street, where "villages" from ten agricultural regions have been reconstructed, and to which authentic village houses have been transferred. Two villages are already completed — village No. 3 from the upper Tisza region and village No. 10 from northwest Hungary. The others are in the process of being built. This fascinating museum is spread over a green park on an area of 116 acres with a stream running through the middle.

You can reach the Open-Air Museum by car or on foot from the city center or by the bus which leaves from platform No. 8 every hour, from the bus station alongside the railroad station (*HEV*). The museum is open from April-October, 9am-5pm (entrance tickets are sold until 4:30pm).

On weekends and during the Szentendre Days Festival (Szentendrei Teátrum) in June and July, the town bustles with visitors, Hungarians and foreigners, and the same is true during the Spring Festival, when several performances are held here.

From Szentendre to Visegrád

The route north from Szentendre passes through **Leányfalu**, a vacation spot located 7 kms from the city. Here we find the home of the Hungarian writer Zsigmond Móricz (1942-1979), a ferry to Szentendre Island, and a good camp site with vacation bungalows and other amenities which is open during the entire tourist season (1 Szabadság tér, tel. 23-154).

Visegrád

The small town of Visegrád, with less than 3,000 inhabitants, is located 24 kms from Szentendre. It is proud of its glorious past, when it served as the residence of the Hungarian kings. The cliff which rises above the Danube and the fortress which was built at its summit are breathtakingly beautiful, and they are among the most impressive sites in the Danube Bend region.

The tourist information bureau is at 3a Fő utca (tel. 28-330), and next to it is the dependable *Vár* hotel at No. 9 of the same street (tel.28-264).

Above the town, on the way to the hilltop is a good 3-star hotel called *Silvanus* (tel. 28-311), and an excellent wild game restaurant opposite the campsite at the summit of the hill, *Nagyvillam Vendéglő* (tel. 28-070). The restaurant serves excellent venison with side dishes of croquettes, steamed plums, and rice in blackberry sauce (*Ozfilé krokettel áfonyával*), and has a splendid view of the cliff.

What to see

A path leads from the restaurant to the highest spot on the cliff, **Nagy-Villám Towers**, which is open during the daylight hours of the tourist season, and provides a good view of the area. Opposite, in Mogyoró-hegy (tel. 28-217) is the *Jurta* campsite with bungalows and other amenities.

Return via the winding road to the campsite opposite **Visegrad Fortress** (Visegrádi Fellegvár). The fortress protected the royal palace, and the view from it is exciting. A path leads from the campsite through the woods to the observation towers and the restored halls of the fortress.

From the upper fortress, continue on to the lower fortress, whose construction was ordered in the middle of the 13th century by King Béla IV, with the intention of ensuring control of the Danube Bend. Charles Robert of Anjou made the fortress his place of residence in 1326, and built his palace there. Nine years later (1335), the kings of central Europe met in this palace for the Congress of Visegrád, which dealt with policy, territorial rights, and trade in the region. The palace of Charles Robert served as the base for expansion of the building, begun by Sigismund and continued later by King Matthias Corvinus, who built a magnificent palace there. Remains of the palace can still be seen here despite the destruction caused by time and by the Turkish occupation.

At the entrance to the palace (27 Fő utca), near the Danube boat dock, is the reception hall. From here, we continue on a tour of the palace, some of whose royal halls have been carefully restored. The palace was built on four levels. Take note of the well made of red marble on the second level and the Lions' Fountain on the fourth level.

The palace was very luxurious (so much so that the emissary of the Pope wrote the Vatican in 1438 that he was at "Visegrád Palace, a real Garden of Eden"). Also, very impressive is a visit to the **King Matthias Museum** (Mátyás Király Múzeum)

In the Royal Palace — Visegrád

at 29 Fő utca. Many items found at the palace are kept here and at **Solomon's Tower** (Salamon tornya) next to the river fortress (Vizibástya). These were part of the fortifications of the royal palace, and a wall connected them to the upper fortress. Solomon's Tower is named after the king who was imprisoned in the 11th century by his heir, King Ladislas, in Visegrád Fortress (many years before the existence of the tower).

Another historical site next to the palace is the **royal hunting lodge** at 41 Fő utca (Középkori Királyi palota kotara), located in a large structure built in Baroque style two hundred years ago for the comfort of the king and his guests. The museums and historical sites are open to visitors Tues.-Sun. during the tourist season from 9am-5pm.

From Visegrád to Esztergom

From Visegrád you can take walking trips in the Pilis mountains, in the range of hills known as Visegrádi Hegyek (see the section devoted to the Pilis mountains further on in this chapter), or join a horseback or pony trip, organized by the *Dunatours* tourist bureau. Seven kilometers west, along the Danube, is the **Dömös campsite**, where there are remains of a monastery from the 11th century, as well as the estuary of the Malom River. This stream is one of the tributaries of the Danube and serves as the point of departure and return for several footpaths in the Pilis mountains.

Esztergom

Esztergom is about 70 kms from Budapest, on the left bank of the "Bend." Esztergom has served as a very important Roman Catholic religious center, ever since Prince Géza adopted Christianity for himself (and for all Hungary) in the 10th century AD. The city also served as the capital of ancient Hungary, and it was here that King István, son of Géza, was crowned the first king of Hungary. Today it has about 30,000 inhabitants.

Esztergom was already settled in the 1st century AD by the Romans. They called the city Salvo Mansio, and for a while, the Roman Caesar Marcus Aurelius resided here. However, the centrality and importance of the city belong mainly to the time when Prince Géza selected it for his seat of government, in 970 AD.

Hungarian kings who lived at Esztergom continued to develop the city during the Middle Ages, receiving as their guests the Christian kings of Europe who were enroute to the Holy Land, during the Crusades in the 12th century. After the Mongol invasion in the 13th century, the center of government was moved to Visegrád and to Buda, but the Archbishop of Hungary, the head of the Catholic Church in the country, remained in the city. It continued to be an ecclesiastical center despite the Turkish conquest and other disasters, and it has remained so until today.

Opposite Esztergom the Danube divides, forming a branch called Kis Duna (small Danube) which creates a green island. The island is connected to this impressive city via several bridges. One of them, Kossuth híd, leads to the center of the lower city.

Tourist services

The tourist information bureau *Komturist* is located at No. 13 Séchenyi tér (tel. 484), and the *Express* agency, specializing in inexpensive hostels, is located at No. 7 in the same square. The local post office is there as well.

Food and lodging

The *Esztergom* hotel, on Primás Island opposite the city, is the best hotel in town (tel. 81-68). Two dependable cheaper hotels are the *Fürdő*, centrally located at 14 Bajcsy-Zsilinszky utca (tel. 292) which also has a good restaurant, and the *Volán* Hotel (2 József Attila tér, tel. 271). *Turistaszálló* offers dark, unpleasant rooms at low prices (8 Dobozi M. utca, tel. 8428). For the same money it would be preferable to stay in one of the private rooms which can be rented via the tourist agencies or the local *IBUSZ* office (Mártírok utca, tel. 100).

Among the good restaurants in town, it is worthwhile mentioning *Hal szcsárda* on Primás Island and *Kispipa* restaurant, considered the best in the city, at 19 Kossuth Lajos utca, not far from the *Komturist*.

What to see

Szent István tér is located in front of the **Cathedral** (Bazilika), and from here we start our tour of the royal citadel of Esztergom. Construction of the cathedral, the largest in Hungary, was completed in 1869 by Hild József after 45 years of work. This cathedral, which is of grand dimensions, was built in the Classical style on the site of a small place of worship from the eleventh century. It is 118 meters long, 40 meters wide, and its dome reaches a height of over 70 meters. Legend has it that Beethoven offered to conduct his *Missa Solemnis* at the dedication ceremony of the church, but the construction took so much longer than planned, that it was finally Liszt who was honored with the performance of his *Esztergom Mass* at the opening.

The entrance to the cathedral is to the left. There, tickets are sold which are valid for the church cellars (Altemplom) and for the church treasury (kincstár) as well. In the cathedral entrance, on the right, stairs lead to cellars. From here, you can get a better idea of the size of the building. Note the huge statues and the tombs of several archbishops who served in the church. After visiting the cellar, go up to the cathedral to see the huge painting over the central pulpit, the work of the Italian artist Grigoletti, who was greatly influenced by Titian.

Esztergom — Castle Hill

A stairway in the northwest corner of the shrine leads to the church treasury with its rich store of religious objects of silver, gold, and precious stones from the 11th century onward. With its vestments of the archbishops and its priestly scepters, gilded and inlaid with precious stones — it is the most valuable religious collection in Hungary! Church treasures, buried in cellars for hundreds of years, are now on display from April-October, Tues.-Sun. between 9am-5pm. During the tourist season, organ concerts take place in the cathedral several times a week.

South of the church is the **Chapel** (Bakócz Kápolna), made of red marble, built in Renaissance style in 1506. 350 years after the cathedral was built, the chapel was moved stone by stone and reassembled alongside the grand cathedral.

The **Esztergom Historical Museum** (Esztergomi Vármúzeum) is located to the left of the cathedral. Its exhibits are in the halls of the ancient royal fortress. Open all year round Tues.-Sun. from 9am-5pm. Return to István Square next to the ancient wall to have a look at the massive fortifications.

After visiting Castle Hill, walk along Bajcsy-Zsilinszky Street in the direction of the **Christian Museum** (Keresztény Múzeum) at

2 Berényi Zsigmond utca (open Tues.-Sun., during the tourist season 10am-6pm, and during the rest of the year 11am-5pm). This impressive museum, with one of the most outstanding collections in Hungary, is located in the Archbishop's Palace and includes art works from the 13th century to the 19th century which were gathered by the Church. The museum has an impressive collection of Italian paintings, one of the largest of its kind outside Italy, as well as Hungarian sculpture and French and Dutch hand-woven rugs.

Market enthusiasts can visit the **City Market** at the top of Zalka Máte Street, next to the bus station. Here, villagers gather from all over the region to sell their products.

Pilis Mountains

These mountains are more renowned for their wooded landscapes than for the height of their summits (the highest is only 700 meters). There are several canyons and limestone caves worth visiting, and a hike takes only 3-4 hours. Don't go off on your hike without a detailed map, such as the *A pilis turistatérképe* map, which is sold at the best bookstores on Váci utca in Budapest and at the Esztergom Historical Museum.

Begin your hike from the scenic observation point at a height of 699 meters at Dobogókő next to *Nimród* hotel (tel. 27-644), which is a pleasant hotel for those spending a night in the area. For those travelling by train from Esztergom to Budapest, we recommend stopping here to enjoy the view. The lookout point is at the intersection of footpaths which cross the forested hills. A popular and quite short route (about 3 hours of walking) is the path which descends from the summit to the Ram Cliff. From there, turn north along the Malom tributary which goes as far as Dömős.

Another, longer route, starting at the same lookout point in Dobogókő, will lead you east to the Bükkös River. From there, turn north with the path leading to Kovac canyon, to the town of Pilisszentlászló, and to the ruins of the monastery next to it.

In this area there are several hotels and guest houses for tourists (*Turistaház*). During the tourist season, if you want to stay overnight at any of the hotels in the area, reservations must be made in advance, via the tourist agencies, to avoid arriving at an isolated hotel only to find that it is full to capacity.

The east bank

The east bank is less interesting and attractive than the west. The only city which attracts tourists here is **Vác**, about 34 kms north of Budapest. The city developed at an important crossroads during the Roman period, when it served as the gateway to the "land of the Barbarians" east of the Danube. If you include this city in your tour, make use of the services of the *Dunatours* tourist bureau (14 Széchenyi utca, tel. 10-940) and visit the cathedral built between 1763-1777, in centrally located Konsantin Square.

Continue north on Köztársaság Street via 15 Március tér, to **Victory Gate**, built by the Bishop Migazzi in 1764 to commemorate the visit of the Austrian Empress Maria Theresa. Additional sites, of less interest, are the Vak Bottyán Historical Museum (4 Múzeum utca) and other churches in town which were built, for the most part, in Baroque style during the 18th century.

From Vác we continue along the Danube to **Nagymaros**, formerly a quiet village opposite Visegrád. A controversial dam is now being erected on the Danube beside it, making it a subject for much discussion and disagreement among Hungarians.

The episode began with an agreement signed between Hungary and Czechosovakia to build a dam next to Nagymaros, which would supply electricity to both countries. Austria invested the money, and work began in 1986. More and more voices were raised against building the dam because of the anticipated ecological damage. International experts confirmed that construction of the dam might lead to destructive results — obliteration of the natural environment of animals and plants, and even inundation of populated cities along the banks of the river.

Today, the Hungarian leadership is unclear about its policy in the matter of the dam. Inasmuch as construction has already begun, cancellation of the project would create an international dispute and would entail payment of sums beyond the limited capacity of the country's treasury to provide. In 1989, the Hungarian government decided to freeze the project, with the intention of cancelling it completely.

After a visit to the controversial dam, continue on to the picturesque town of **Zebegény** (8 kms from Nagymaros) from which the railroad leaves for Czechoslovakia and the border town of **Szob**. In the **Börzsöny Museum** in Szob (14 Hámán Kató utca) emphasis is placed on exhibits of arts and crafts and rural dress.

The Börzsöny Mountains are higher and wilder than the Pilis hills on the opposite bank. Tourist services such as restaurants, hotels and guest houses are very limited. Making detailed plans of the route of your trip in advance is a must. You can reach the quiet villages of Nagybörzsöny and Kőspallag by car.

Northern Transdanubia

The Danube cuts across Hungary from north to south. Western Hungary is the region of Transdanubia, which has been continuously settled since the period of the Roman Empire, and was then called the province of Pannonia. During the Turkish occupation, when the forces of the Hungarian monarchy retreated from most regions of the country, a "Hungarian Monarchy" was established in this region, which, in effect, was the front line of battle of the Austrian Hapsburg dynasty.

Northern Transdanubia is bordered by Budapest in the east, Lake Balaton region in the south, and the Austrian and Czechoslovakian borders in the north and west. It is a flat country, rich in ancient cities, agricultural regions, and quiet pastoral landscapes. The roads in the area are good and its tourist amenities well developed. Many travellers who drive directly from Vienna to Budapest miss out on some of the most beautiful tourist spots in the country.

From Budapest to Győr

The international highway E75/E60 goes northwest from Budapest to the Austrian-Czechoslovakian-Hungarian border junction. This wide highway takes you — after 55 kms — to the industrial city of **Tatabanya**. The Turul statue of the legendary eagle-like bird (which was the symbol of the ancient Magyars) was built in 1896 on a hilltop in the city to commemorate 1,000 years of Hungarian occupation. This observation point, which looks out over the green plains of the region, is the most interesting site in this grey coal town, of about 80,000 inhabitants. Alongside the city are the ruins of the **Vitány Castle** (Vitány Vár), built in Gothic style over 600 years ago. The ruins are not very attractive, but give you the opportunity to stretch your muscles in a natural setting. A pleasant walk of 3 kms should start at the village of **Vértessomoló**, which may be reached by car or by local bus. The village of Vértesszőlős, about 10 kms north of here, made the headlines during the 1960's, when the remains of one of the earliest pre-historic settlements in the world (its estimated age is about 500,000 years) were found there.

Fourteen kms north of Tatabánya is **Tata**, a city whose beginnings were in the Roman period and which today has 25,000 inhabitants. The city was built on the northern shore

NORTHERN TRANSDANUBIA

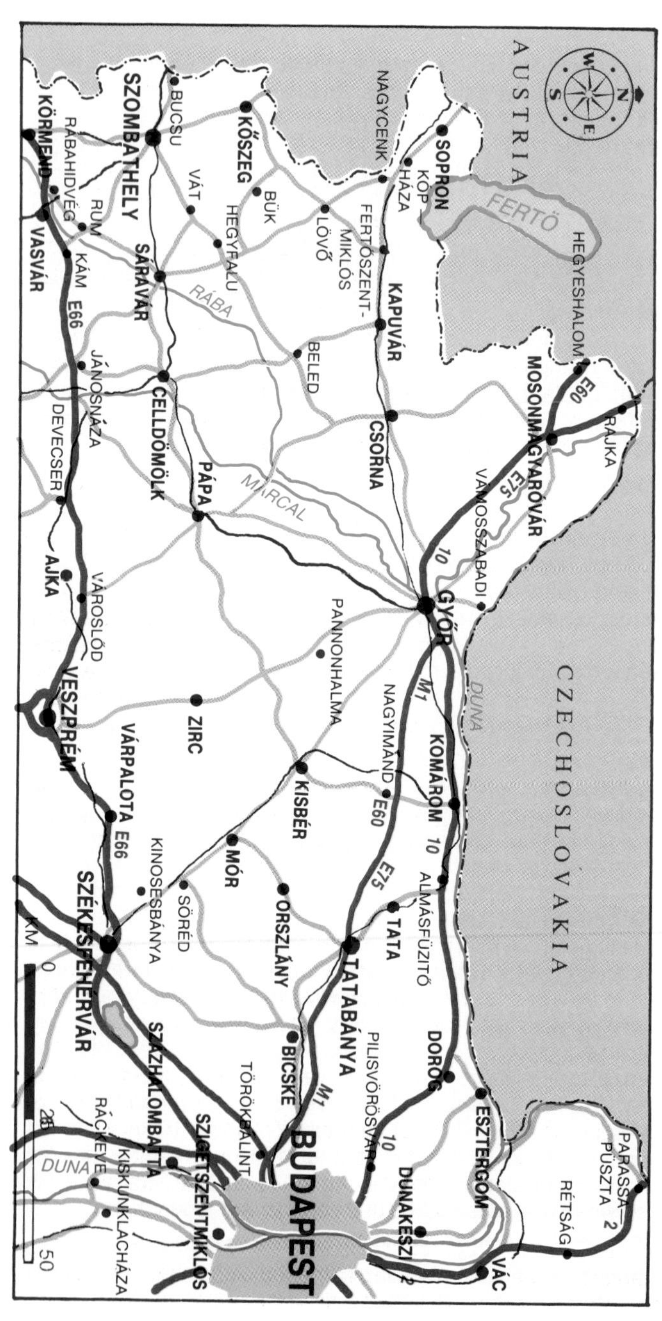

of the "ancient lake" (Oregtó). The **Ancient Castle** (Oregvár) in the center of town, on the shore of the lake, is the main local attraction. This castle was first built in Gothic style during the 14th century. It was restored in 1822 in the Romantic style, after having been destroyed by the Hapsburg dynasty (at the beginning of the 18th century) as punishment for the participation of inhabitants of the region in the revolt led by R kóczi. Today, the castle houses the **Kuny Domonkos Museum**, which contains local pottery and ceramic vessels (open during the tourist season from Tues.-Sun. 10am-6pm. During the rest of the year, the museum closes at 2pm).

Many buildings in the old city were designed in the Baroque style, during the second half of the 18th century according to the plans of the architect Fellner, whose patron was Count Esterházy. If you wish to visit these buildings, go south from the museum in the ancient castle to November 7 tér, to **Esterházy Palace** (Esterházy Kastély), built in 1756. From there, continue on Rákóczi Street to Kossuth Square, where you will find the Catholic Church **Tatai Templom**. This tour is recommended for architecture enthusiasts only.

The Ethnographic Museum in the city, devoted to the German minority (*Nemzétiségi Néprajzi Múzeum*) and the water stations built by Fellner sound more interesting in the literature of the local *Komturist* tourist bureau (9 Ady Endre utca, tel. 81-805) than they are in reality. You may want to end the tour with a visit to *Barátok Asztala* restaurant at 1 Bartók Béla utca.

Those in possession of a visa to Czechoslovakia can continue from Tata to the border town of **Komárom**, next to the border crossing. Others, will have to continue on to Győr.

Győr

Győr is one of the oldest cities in Hungary. The Romans built an important city at this site called Arrabona, which developed around the fortress on **Káptalan Hill**. It was abandoned after the Mongol invasion in the 4th century AD until the Magyar conquest. Renewed growth of the city brought with it the construction of the cathedral in the first half of the 11th century. Also, during the 13th century, the right to exact a tax from those passing through the region. The appearance of the city center today has been influenced by the spurt of building and renovation, in the Baroque style, which began in the 17th and 18th centuries. Today, the city has 130,000 inhabitants. It is an industrial town, quite drab, but its chief pride is its famous dance troupe.

Danube tributaries — the Mason, the Rábca, and the Rába divide the city into three areas. Káptalan Hill, east of the Rába River, is the center of the old city, around which the city developed. On the other side of the Rába River, where it meets the Mason, are the city's famous bath-houses. The island in the center of the river, west of the old city, serves as a tranquil green park.

How to get there

Győr is located midway between Budapest and Vienna, 125 kms from the Hungarian capital. Many busses from Budapest, Vienna, Sopron and Lake Balaton reach the bus station in Győr, on Hunyadi utca, south of the city center. Local trains come from Budapest and the other cities nearby, several times a day. (The train station is near the bus station).

Tourist services

The *IBUSZ* tourist information bureau is at 29-31 Tanácsközt rsaság (tel. 14-224). The local tourist agency is *Ciklamen Tourist* at 12 Jókay utca (tel.15-122). The local post office is on Bajcsy Zsilinszki Street, east of the corner of Czuczor Gergely Street in the center of town.

Other tourist attractions in Győr are boating and fishing on the Danube tributaries, organized by *Ciklámen Tourist.*

Food and lodging

Budget-minded tourists should rent a room in a private home. Such rooms can be found via the tourist bureaus already mentioned. Those with less limited budgets can certainly take rooms at the modern *Rába* Hotel (34 Arpád utca, tel. 15-533), which also has a good restaurant. An excellent campsite with comfortable bungalows (*Kiskútligeti Camping*, tel. 18-896) is open during the tourist season.

What to see

A good place to begin a tour of the city is Köztársaság tér, on the bank of the Rába river at the foot of Castle Hill. In the square, the **Carmelite Church** (Karmelita Templom) stands out. It is the most beautiful church in the city, built in 1725 in the Baroque style. Also of interest is the **Castle Museum** (Bástya Múzeum) at No. 5 in the square with Roman ruins (open during the tourist season Tues.-Sun. from 10am-6pm).

From the lovely square, go up Káptalan Street to the fortified hill with Martinovics tér at its center, where the **Cathedral** was built. The first to fortify the hill were the Romans who built a fortress where the legionnaires had lived. Around the fortress, the Roman city of Arrabona developed.

Looking at the cathedral may make your head spin, because of the many styles and numerous renovations it has undergone. Construction began, apparently, in the 11th century and continued until the beginning of the 13th century. A **Gothic chapel** (Hédervάry Kάpolna) was added next to the cathedral at the beginning of the 15th century. In it are preserved parts of the skull of King Stephen I (reigned 997-1038) to whom the cathedral is dedicated. After the destruction caused by the Turkish conquest, the church was renovated in the Baroque style (in the middle of the 17th century), and 200 years later, its facade was redone in the neo-Classical style. The most recent renovations were carried out after the Second World War.

West of the cathedral is the **Bishop's Palace** of Győr. It was first built in the 13th century and was renovated in the Baroque style in the 17th century. The home of the servants of the bishop (at house No. 1 in the square) now serves as a museum of art, in which works of the sculptor Borsos Miklós are exhibited (open Tues.-Sun. from 10am-5pm).

From Martinovics Square it is pleasant to walk through the narrow, winding, old streets to Alkotmány utca. Here, turn left to house No. 4 — a Baroque palace which belonged to the Esterházy family. In 1809 Napoleon was a guest here, while his forces were quelling an uprising of Hungarian noblemen. On the first floor of the palace is the gallery of the **City Museum**, with paintings and additional exhibitions.

Alkotmány utca leads to Széchenyi tér. In the square is the **Benedictine Church** (Bencés Templom), built for the Jesuit Order in 1634, and annexed to the nearby Benedictine monastery, which was built in the 17th century. Note the beautiful paintings of Troger Paul on the ceiling.

There are two museums in Széchenyi tér. At No. 5 is the interesting **Museum of the City's History** from the Roman period onward. The museum is named after the 19th century scholar and researcher **Xantus János** (open on summer Tues.-Sun. from 10am-6pm, in winter it closes one hour earlier). In house No. 9 in the square, **Patika Múzeum**, is a museum in a pharmacy which served the Benedictine monks for hundreds of years. Interest in this museum centers chiefly around its interior design and especially the impressive paintings above the heads of the tourists (open Mon., Tues., Thurs., and Fri. from 8am-5pm, on Wed. from 1pm-5pm, and on Sun., from 9am-1pm).

Special events

If you like ballet, don't miss a performance of the city's modern dance troupe, which is one of the finest and most famous dance

Győr — center of the old city

troupes in Europe. (For more information contact the local tourist bureaus.) Other cultural activities take place during the local music festival in June-July.

Pannonhalma monastery

The **Pannonhalma Monastery** is one of the best preserved in the country, 20 kms southeast of Győr. It can be reached by road No. 82 or by bus, which leaves Győr several times a day. The monastery sits on a hilltop 280 meters high, with a good view

Pannonhalma — ceiling of the monastery

of the surrounding plains. Next to the iron gate is a tourist bureau, from which you can join a tour in an organized group. Often, people from the monastery are also willing to permit individual tourists to enter, and a monk may even guide you around its various collections.

Pannonhalma Monastery is the center of the Benedictine Church in the country, and the head of the order lives here. The first structure was built by Prince Géza in 996, and it was completed by his son, Stephen I. Monastery buildings were rebuilt many times since then. The foundations of the present church, Szt. Márton Bazilika, were first laid in 1224 in Romanesque style. The only remains from that time are those of the *crypt*, the underground hall underneath the church. 17th century renovations (in the Baroque style) and construction work, including the building of the high tower in the 19th century (in neo-Classical style), have given the monastery its present form.

The monastery contains many collections gathered by the monks over the past thousand years. The most outstanding collection here is in the library built by King Ladislas. Today, it has over 300,000 volumes. Its collections include the first written evidence of words and names in Hungarian (from 1055) in documents concerning construction of the Benedictine monastery in Tihany on the shores of Lake Balaton.

From Győr to border crossings

Road E60/E75 continues from Győr northwest for 38 kms to **Mosonmagyaróvár**. There are 30,000 inhabitants in this town. You can visit the beautiful fortress which was built in the middle of the 13th century between the tributaries of the Lajta River as well as the **Hanság Museum** (open Tues.-Sun. from 10am-6pm during the tourist season; during the rest of the year it closes at 5pm) which is devoted to the history of the city and its people.

Here, the road separates to the north and to the west. The road north, E75, leads to the Czechoslovakian border in Rajka, 18 kms away. Route E60 leads to Hegyeshalom, 13 kms away at the Austrian border. The border crossings are open 24 hours a day. Visitors coming to Hungary can acquire entrance visas, change money, and receive basic information about the country at *IBUSZ* offices at the border.

From Győr to Sopron

Route 85 goes west from Győr, passing Csorna and Kapuvár, before turning north to **Fertőd**, about 55 kms from Győr.

Fertőd was a quiet village until 1760, when construction work began on the large palace of Miklós Esterházy, who was head of the famous family. At that time, the village was called Esterháza in honor of the family. Here, Miklós Esterházy built one of the family's palaces which was referred to as the "Hungarian Versailles." The palace had 126 rooms and was built in the shape of a horseshoe. It included a large concert hall, in which Joseph Haydn, house musician for thirty years, conducted the works he had written. (Haydn's house, which was next to the palace, burnt down at the beginning of the 20th century). The beautiful palace was built in the Baroque style.

Following Miklós' death in 1790, the palace was neglected.

After the Second World War, it was renovated and the gardens opened to the public.

During the summer months, concerts are held at the palace. Compositions of Mozart and Haydn are the main fare. In one of the wings of the palace, a hotel was opened (very expensively priced). Because of the great demand, those wanting accommodations here need to make reservations in advance at travel agencies or at the palace itself (tel. 45-971).

The *Haydn* restaurant on the main street in the village is the place to go for a meal and a rest after touring the palace. A local bus connects Fertőd and Sopron, which is 27 kms to the west.

Sopron

The city of 60,000 inhabitants, is the second most important tourist center in the country (after Budapest). The city's proximity to the Austrian border (only 7 kms away), atracts many Austrians who come for shopping. Their influence is considerable, and the German language is widely used.

The old city of Sopron is full of tourists almost all year round, and this detracts from its charm, and tries the patience of the local inhabitants. Tourists are often approached by Hungarians offering to change their money at a rate much higher than the official rate. Nevertheless, a visit to the old city with its many impressive historical buildings is a must.

History of the city

Settlement here apparently began during the days of the Celts, but the city became more important only when the fortified waystation of Scarabantia was established on the ancient Byzantine trade route from the eastern Roman Empire to Vienna. The city was designed in the shape of a fortified ellipse, inside which large public buildings were erected. From all these structures, only remnants of the surrounding wall remain.

After the Roman period, the city lost its importance until the establishment of Magyar rule.

In the last quarter of the 13th century, Sopron was accorded the status of a city, bringing with it renewed construction in the Gothic style. One of the buildings erected at that time was the Benedictine Church (Kecske Templom) in which Hungarian kings were crowned during the 16th and 17th centuries. Because it was never conquered by the Turks nor bombed in World War II, the city remained intact.

More than 350 historical buildings and monuments are found in

Fertőd — Esterházy palace

Sopron, which possesses the greatest concentration of historical sites in the country.

Geographical location

The old city (Belváros), located at the site of the ancient Roman city, is surrounded by Lenin Körút. The boulevard forms a horseshoe shape, and most of the interesting tourist sites in the city are found within it. Fő tér in the center of the horseshoe is the heart of the historical city, while Széchenyi tér is located at the open end of the horseshoe. You can reach the center of town from the train station on Mátyás Király Street. The bus station is located northwest of the center of the old city, on Lackner Kristóf Street.

How to get there

By train: five trains leave Budapest daily for Sopron from the southern railroad station (Déli pu). The trip takes two hours. Those coming from Győr can catch this train which also stops there. The international train to Austria makes a daily connection between Sopron and Wiener-Neustadt in Austria.

By bus: The connection between Budapest and Sopron is

not very satisfactory, since the busses go via Szombathely, lengthening the trip considerably. The bus from Győr to Sopron makes many stops during the 87 kms between the two cities.

By car: From Győr take road 85, and from Lake Balaton take road 84. From Vienna, road 16 takes you to the border crossing at Klingenbach, only half a kilometer west of Sopron.

Tourist services

Ciklámen is at 8 Obavona tér (tel. 12-040), next to the railroad station. The *IBUSZ* agency (41 Lenin körút, tel. 13-281) will help you find accomodations.

The *Express* agency, which serves young people, is located on the way from the train station to the center, at 7 Mátyás Kiraly utja (tel. 12-024). The central post office is far from the center of town on Mikoviny Street, west of the train station.

Food and lodging

The limited selection of hotels and the large number of tourists mean that you are well advised to reserve a hotel room here several weeks in advance of your visit. Those who can't or don't want to make advance reservations, will need a room in a private home.

Palatinus hotel, a 3-star hotel, is located in an attractive building in the center of the old city. (23 Uj utca, tel. 11-395).

Sopron hotel, also a 3-star hotel, is north of the center in a quiet area (4 Fövényverem utja, tel. 14-254).

Pannónia hotel, the only 2-star hotel in the city, although in need of repair, is comfortable, centrally located (75 Lenin körút, tel. 12-180) and its friendly atmosphere makes for a pleasant stay.

The hostels (*Turistaszállo*) at Uj utca (tel. 12-185) and at 4 Ferenczi utca (tel. 12-228) are quite noisy, so, either a room in a private home or in the inexpensive bungalows at the *Lövér* campsite in the rather distant Pocsi-Domb neighborhood would be preferable.

Among the city center restaurants: *Kékfrankos* at 12 Széchenyi tér, *Gambrinus* at Uj utca, and *Generális* at Fő tér. These restaurants are more pretentious (and expensive) than those found along Lenin Blvd., where you can eat piping hot goulash soup at bargain rates.

The *Szelmalom* restaurant (4 Fraknói utca) is also a coffee-house and is a good place to get a light meal. The bistros scattered along Lenin Blvd. (at No. 7, No. 25, No. 104) are also good places to find inexpensive meals. A visit to a typical wine cellar (2 Hátsokápu utca) is just the thing for an evening of wine and snacks.

What to see

The old city

Enter the old city via the outer gate (Előkapu) from Lenin körút and walk to the **Fire Tower** (Tűztorony), the structure which stands out most in the city and has become its emblem. The tower was built in three parts: the bottom part is round, built in Romanesque style during the Middle Ages from stones of the Roman wall; the middle part, octagonal, was built during the 16th century in a Renaissance spirit; and the Baroque dome was added only at the end of the 17th century. The tower is 61 meters high. In 1921, the **Gate of Loyalty** was added to commemorate the decision of the inhabitants to join Hungary rather than Austria. You can climb the 124 steps up the tower to the observation point, which affords a good view. Open to visitors from April-October, Tues.-Sun. from 10am-6pm; from November-March, the tower closes at 4pm. The entrance ticket to the tower also includes entrance to the historical museum in the tower cellar, containing Roman relics found there.

Fő tér at the foot of the Fire Tower is most impressive. Many of its museums are located in homes dating from the 15th century on. Next to the tower, at No. 8, is the home of the honourable **Storno family**, built in Renaissance style, and considered to be the most beautiful palace in the city. One of their friends who was a guest here was the legendary King Matthias. Baroque style additions have been integrated into this palace without disturbing the harmony of its appearance. Here, you can see art treasures collected by the family, including many paintings and sculptures.

No. 7 on the square serves as a small museum for stone engravings from the 17th and 18th centuries, including sculptures and reliefs found in the city. No. 6 is **Fabricius House**, built in Baroque style on Roman foundations. In its cellar remains from the Roman period were found, and they are exhibited along with other archeological findings. Open Tues.-Sun. from 10am-6pm, and during the rest of the year until 5 pm. Other important houses in the square are house No. 3, **Gambrinus House**, used as the city hall during the Middle Ages, and a small **Pharmacy Museum** (Patika Múzeum) at No. 2, whose hall is of more interest than the items exhibited in it.

Goat Church (Kecske Templom), at the corner of Templom Street, got its name from the legend which says that the money raised in order to build it was brought by a shepherd whose goats found a gold treasure in the fields. But this lovely church, built in the 13th century, remains the most beautiful Gothic church in the country. In the 17th century, some of the Hungarian kings were crowned here.

Continue southward on Templom utca. At No. 2, in a palace which belonged to the Esterházy family, is an interesting **Museum of the History of Mines** in the region. The houses on this ancient street are built mostly in the Baroque style. From here, we turn left to the short Fegivertár Street, which ends at Orsolya tér. At No. 5 in the square is the **History of the Guilds Museum**, in a restored building (Lábasház).

On the streets branching out from Orsolya tér are many inviting attractions for the visitor to explore. Hátsó-Kapu Street is the rear exit gate of the old city, and it leads from the square to Lenin körút. At No. 2 is **Ceasar House**, where you can visit an ancient wine cellar which has been in use for hundreds of years. Szt. György utca which leads from Orsolya Square to the central square is famous for its beautiful **Erdödy Palace** (at No. 16), built in Rococo style. As you pass by, take a look at **Eggenberger House** (No. 12) with its lovely yard.

Uj utca, running parallel to Szt. György, was the Jewish Quarter. At No. 22 is the **New Synagogue** (Uj Zsinagoga), built in the 15th century. In it is a small Jewish museum (open April-November Mon., Wed.-Sun. from 9am-5pm, and until 4pm during the rest of the year).

Outside the old city

At Május 1 tér is the most important museum in the city — **Franz Liszt Museum** (Liszt Ferenc Múzeum). During the tourist season, it is open Tues.-Sun. from 10am-6pm, and during the rest of the year until 5 pm. The museum contains an archeological collection which documents the history of the region, and an art collection. A special exhibit is devoted to the composer, for whom the museum has been named. Franz Liszt began his musical career in this city, performing piano recitals.

On the other side of the old city, at 11 Balfi út, is the **Zetti-Langer collection** which includes weapons, delicate porcelains, and other objects of beauty. It is open daily from 10am-12noon only.

After visiting the museum, continue to nearby Pozsonyi utca to the **Church of Saint Michael** (Szent Mihály Templom). Construction of this church was begun in the 13th century, making it one of the oldest churches in the city. House No. 9 on the same street is referred to as the **House of the two Moors** (Két Mór Ház), after the Moorish-style decorations over the two spiral pillars standing at the gate.

SOPRON

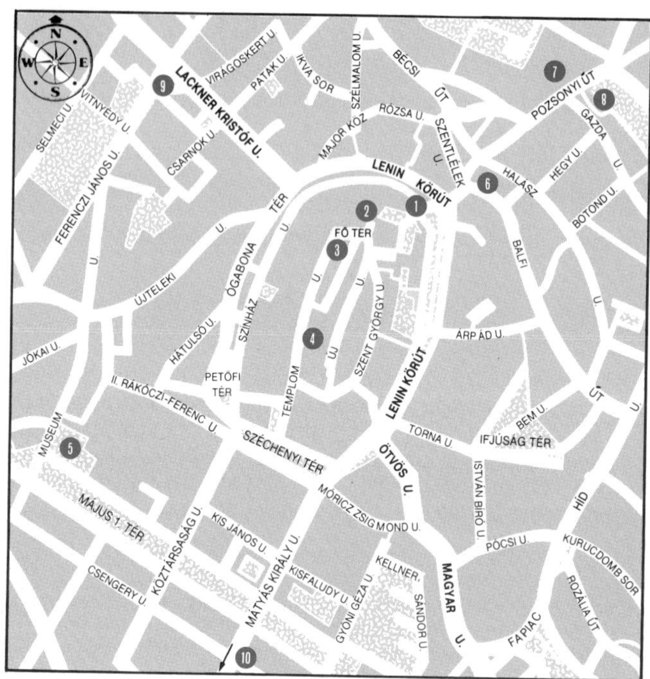

Index
1. Elókapu Gate
2. Fire Lookout Tower
3. Goat Church
4. Synagogue and Museum
5. Franz Liszt Museum
6. Zettl Langer collection
7. House of the two Moors
8. St. Michael's Church
9. Central bus station
10. To the railway station

A pleasant walk can be taken through the Löverek Hills southwest of the city (information and maps at the local tourist bureaus).

The **Fertőrákos Quarries** are located about 10 kms northeast of Sopron, beside Lake Fertő. The Romans began digging here and carting the huge stone slabs to building sites in Transdanubia. The quarry remained in use throughout Hungarian history. During the Second World War, the Nazis made use of this protected spot to set up an underground factory.

The land is blessed with abundance...

Sopron — Fire Lookout Tower

During the "*Sopron Weeks*" Festival, concerts, operas, and plays are performed at the quarry.

Special events

During the Spring Festival in Budapest, some of the events take place in Sopron, within the framework of the local Spring Festival. The Sopron music festival, "Sopron Weeks," which takes place from the middle of June to the middle of July, offers an abundance of concerts and folklore performances (a booklet with details of the festival events is available at the tourist bureaus). To end the tourist season, a Grape-harvest Festival takes place in Sopron during September.

Kőszeg

50 kms south of Sopron is the pleasant town of Kőszeg, with 15,000 inhabitants. Busses to this quiet town leave Sopron hourly. You can also come by train from Szombathely.

We begin our tour of Kőszeg in Köztársaság tér. Towering over the square is the **Sacred Heart Church**, built in neo-Gothic style on the ruins of an ancient Gothic church from the 15th century. Here, we also find the small *Irottkő* hotel (No. 4 in the square, tel. 333), which is the best hotel in town, the *IBUSZ* tourist bureau (tel. 336), and some restaurants.

A narrow lane leading off the square will bring us to **Heroes' Gate** (Hősi Kapu), the entranceway to the fortified city — the heart of Kőszeg and its old city. The heroes referred to a small force of garrison soldiers led by Jurisics Miklós, who by their heroic stubborn resistance for almost a month, managed to hold off the mighty Turkish forces who stormed across Europe in 1532. The gate was built in 1932 to commemorate the battle.

After passing through the Gate, we find ourselves in Jurisics tér, named after the commander of the troops. At its center is the Gothic church **Szt. Jákos**, built in 1403. Nearby, behind it, is the less impressive **Szt. Imre Church**, built in Baroque style in the 17th century. Also gracing the square are house No. 8, which housed the **City Hall**, and is adorned with colorful wall paintings and, alongside it, in the square, is the **General's House** (Tábornok Ház) (at No. 6), built in the 17th century on the foundation of two separate older houses. From the square, Rájnis József Street leads to the castle.

Jurisics Castle (Jurisics Vár) was built in 1263 and reenforced several times in the next few centuries, when it served as a strategic fortified position in border and land disputes between Hungarian kings and neighboring Austrian noblemen. The Turks who arrived with 200,000 soldiers in 1532 tried to conquer the castle, in which 1,000 garrison soldiers were entrenched, under the command of Jurisics Miklós. The courageous resistance of the Hungarian soldiers, along with the very strong fortifications, held the Turks up for a month and caused them such serious casualties and such a crisis of morale, that military historians regard this battle as a turning point in halting the Turkish advance in Europe. In the castle museum are relics which document the history of the castle, including the big battle against the Turks (open Tues.-Sun. from 9am-5pm).

The border crossing to Austria is at the western edge of town, across from the Austrian town of Rattersdorf. 24 kms south of Kószeg is Szombathely, which you can reach via road 87.

Szombathely

Szombathely, with about 90,000 inhabitants, is thought to be the oldest city in Hungary. It was founded by the Emperor Claudius in 43 AD, named Savaria, and at the beginning of the 2nd century it was proclaimed capital of the Roman province of Upper Pannonia. At the end of that century the Iseum, the Temple of Isis, the Egyptian goddess of the sun, was dedicated here as part of the ritual brought by the Romans from Egypt. As in many cities of Pannonia, over the centuries, there was a gradual decline and decay of the central government after the fall of the Roman Empire, until the city was burnt down in the Mongol invasion in 1241.

During the Middle Ages, Savaria recovered and again became a large commercial center, as its name (which means "Sabbath place") indicates. After the Second World War, many buildings which had been destroyed by bombing were rebuilt, and archeological excavations were undertaken, unearthing the Egyptian temple as well as other ruins.

How to get there

Szombathely is located 230 kms west of Budapest, and is connected by bus as well as express trains (from Déli railway station). Trains and busses also connect Szombathely to Sopron, Kőszeg, and other towns in the region.

By car you can get to Szombathely on road E66 from Budapest, (changing to road 87 or 86 near the end of the trip), or road E65 from Keszthely at Lake Balaton.

Tourist services

IBUSZ is at 3-5 Savaria utca (tel. 14-141) opposite the Savaria Museum. Two other tourist bureaus next to *IBUSZ* are

Fertőrákos — The Roman Quarries

Express (12 Bajcsy-Zsilinszky utca, tel. 11-238) and the local *Savaria Tourist Agency*, (1 Mártirok tér, tel. 12-384).

Food and lodging

Hotel rooms should be reserved in advance during the tourist season. Prominent hotels include: *Claudius* (39 Bartók Béla Körút, tel. 13-760), expensive and excellent, outside the city center, as well as such dependable and centrally located ones as: the *Isis* (1 Rákóczi utca, tel. 14-990) and the *Savaria* (4 Mártirok tér, tel. 11-440).

You can find less expensive rooms in *Tourist Hotel* (Jókai Park, tel. 14-168), which also has a low-budget hostel by the same name. In addition, you can find reasonably priced rooms in private homes (through local tourist agencies).

Among the restaurants which are found in the center of town

Kőszeg — Captain Jurisics Square

is: *Gyöngyös* (8 Savaria utca, tel. 12-665). In Mártirok tér, there are more restaurants, including a very inexpensive, self-service student restaurant.

What to see

At Berzsenyi tér there are several interesting sites. The most outstanding is the neo-Classical **Cathedral**, whose construction was begun in the 18th century. It was destroyed during the bombing by the American airforce at the end of World War II and was rebuilt. In the cathedral courtyard is a small **Roman garden**, where remains have been uncovered of the St. Quirinus Basilica and of a medieval castle. Of special interest, are mosaic floors (open during the summer Tues.-Sun. from 8am-6pm).

To the right of the cathedral, on the square at No. 3, is the **Bishop's Palace**, and to its left, at No. 1, is the **City Hall**. Next to it (2 Hollán utca) is the **Smidt Museum**, devoted to the somewhat esoteric collections of Smidt Lájos (1903-1975), a compulsive collector of out-of-date items, from old newspapers to antique furniture (open Tues.-Sun. from 10am-6pm).

From the square proceed up Forgó utca to the main square of Szombathely, Köztársaság tér. This charming three-sided square is surrounded with houses with colorfully painted walls. This is an ideal place to stop at one of the coffee-houses and restaurants, before continuing via Bejczy utca to the **Iseum**, the temple dedicated to the Egyptian goddess Isis (2 Rákóczi utca). It has undergone many changes since it was built by the Romans in the 2nd century AD until it was uncovered in archeological excavations during the 1950's. Open Tues.-Sun. from 10am-6pm. Its historical importance makes a greater impression on the visitor than the appearance of the ruins. The best time to visit is during the Summer Festival, when operas are performed nearby.

For more Roman ruins, go to the **Savaria Museum**, (open 10am-6pm), at 9 Kisfaludy Sándor utca. Here, along with works of art, sculptures, and sarcophagi, you can see relics from the Roman Empire which have been uncovered near Szombathely.

A very impressive old **Synagogue** is located at the corner of Ferenc and Zrínyi Ilona Streets.

Trips outside the city

Many visitors come to Szombathely in order to see the nearby **Ják Monastery**. The Romanesque Church in the monastery is one of the loveliest of its kind in the country. It was built in 1256 and renovated many times after having been damaged by wars and natural causes. Notice the western facade, which is the most embellished. You can reach the monastery from the city via road 86 to Perint and from there by the local road.

Special events

During Savaria Festival, in June, many concerts, operas, and other performances are held. Another festival, less interesting, is the Autumn Festival in September-October, at the end of the tourist season.

To Zalaegerszeg and the villages of the Őrség Preserve

South of Szombathely is the Zala District, where the character and atmosphere of Hungarian village life from hundreds of years past has been faithfully preserved. The villages are not museums or reconstructions but rather settlements, in which the old and new intermingle. You can get to the area on road 76.

A crossroads and important city in the area, **Zalaegerszeg** (referred to by its 60,000 inhabitants as Zala), is 54 kms south of Szombathely. A bus leaves every hour.

References to Zala as a market town can be found as far as back as the 13th century. During the Turkish occupation, this was the border between the Ottomans and the Hungarian monarchy, and Zala was even the capital of the kingdom. In spite of its illustrious past, Zala is not a special tourist site, though the **regional museum** (Göcseji Múzeum) in Marx tér, next to Széchenyi tér — the first Open-air museum in the country. is interesting and worth a visit. West of the center of town are reconstructed traditional village buildings.

The **Olajipar Museum** nearby, devoted to the oil industry in the area, is less interesting and doesn't warrant a visit. *Zalatour*, the local tourist agency, is in Kovács tér (tel. 11-443). The **Őrség** district, next to the Austrian border, is a beautiful rural district. Its villages are attractive to tourists looking for a tranquil atmosphere. This visit is not to seek out special sites but rather to walk around and absorb the general atmosphere and appearance of the villages. The village of **Oriszentpéter**, 35 kms to the west, is in the center of the Őrség district. There is a Romanesque church in the village from the 13th century, as well as beautiful homes constructed of wooden beams.

From this village you can continue west for 6 kms and visit the delightful village of **Szalafo**, with its Protestant church, or else continue on to **Velmér**, 17 kms to the south of Oriszentpéter, and visit the Gothic church, famous for its medieval wall paintings.

Central Transdanubia and Lake Balaton

Lake Balaton, located in central Transdanubia, is the main vacation site in the country. To a certain extent, it compensates Hungarians for being so far from sea shores and oceans. The lake is alive with activity throughout the tourist season, from May to October. In recent years, the number of Hungarians coming to vacation here has decreased, because prices have risen.

A visit to the north shore of Lake Balaton gives tourists a chance to explore the Bakony Mountain Range which separates the lake from north Transdanubia. The wooded mountains, the tranquil villages and the ancient towns afford a refreshing change from routine vacations on the shore of the lake and also provide an enjoyable day-trip.

In winter, the area changes its appearance completely, not only as regards the cloudy sky and the grey color dominating everything, but also in the dearth of tourists.

Székesfehérvár

This bustling city of 110,000 was established by the Romans at the beginning of the 1st century AD. According to Hungarian tradition, it was here that Arpád pitched his tent during the conquest of the country at the beginning of the 10th century. The first Magyar king, Stephen, called the city Alba Regia and made it the Hungarian capital. In the 11th century a basilica was built where Hungarian kings were crowned during the next centuries. With the Turkish occupation (1543), many of the city's buildings were destroyed, and the magnificent church became a mosque. After the Turks were driven out, the town's buildings were reconstructed, but the city never regained its position.

How to get there

A number of express trains, including international trains which continue on to Austria and Yugoslavia, reach the city via the Déli railway station in Budapest. The connection to Siófok and Balatonfüred on the lake shore is especially good, and every hour a train leaves from the city to these destinations. The *Volán* bus service from Budapest can also be used.

By private car: road 70 is the slow way to come from Budapest,

LAKE BALATON

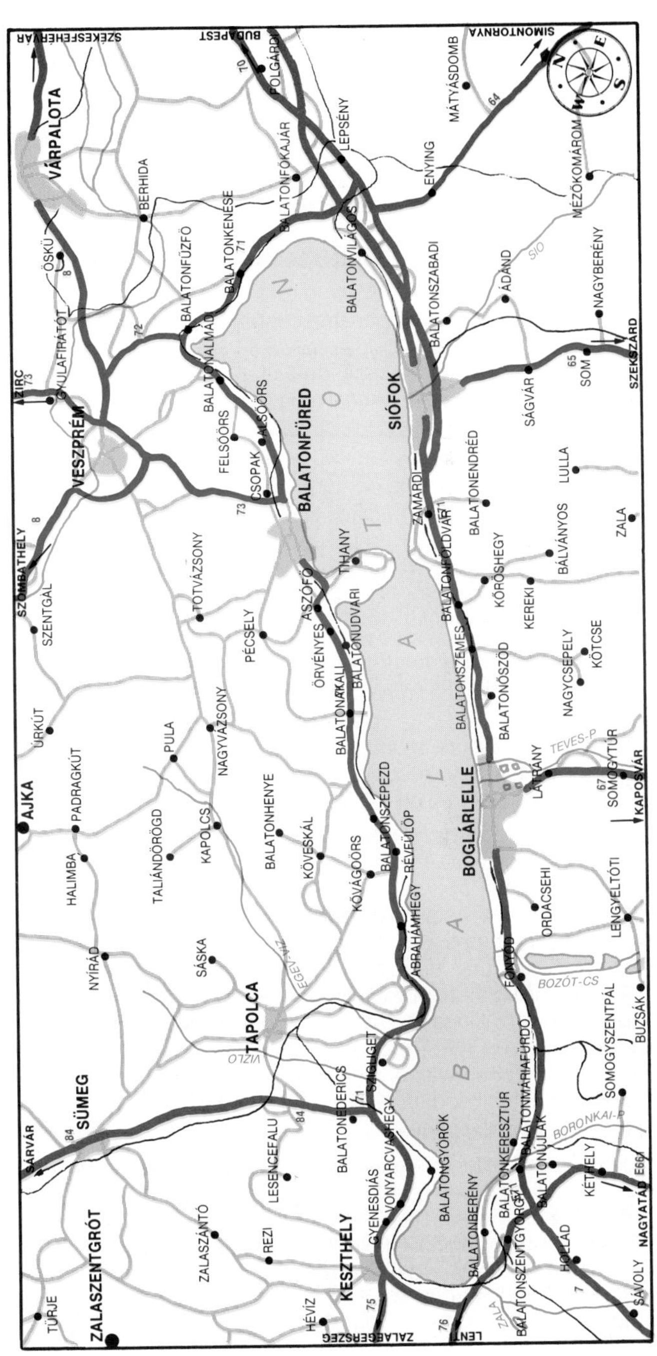

although its route, along the shores of Lake Velence, is much prettier than the route along the E71 (M7) highway (from which you link up with road 70 at the interchange at the entrance to the city). These two roads continue south to the Balaton, while road 8 (E66) leads west to the Bakony Mountains, Szombathely, and the Austrian border.

Tourist services

The local tourist bureau in the center of town is *Albatours*, 6 Szabadság tér (tel. 12-494). *IBUSZ* is located north of the square at 2 Ady Endre utca (tel. 11-510). The office of the *Express* agency is at 4 Rákóczi utca (tel. 14-375).

Food and lodging

Most tourists who visit the city continue on to the shores of Lake Balaton for their overnight stay, therefore are only two hotels in the city. The better one is the centrally located *Alba Regia* (1 Rákóczi utca, tel. 21-295), a 3-star hotel with a swimming pool. The *Velence* hotel, north of the center of town is also very comfortable (10 Március 15 utca, tel. 11-262).

Less expensive rooms are available at the *Türók Udvár* Hostel (2 Jokai utca) or in private homes through the above mentioned travel agencies.

The *Ősfehérvár* restaurant (1 Tancsics Mihaly utca) is considered the best in town, while the chefs at the restaurant in *Velence* hotel, which offers it competition, tend to make generous use of the national spice, paprika.

What to see

The ruins of the ancient **Basilica**, where 38 Hungarian kings were crowned between the 11th century and the Turkish conquest, are the main tourist attraction in the city. These relics, including a burial vault thought to belong to King Stephen I, one of the 18 kings buried here, are exhibited in the **Garden of Ruins** (Romkert) in Szabadság tér. The burial vault thought to belong to Stephen was originally a sarcophagus (according to experts, it actually contains the remains of his son, King Imre). Open from 9am-5pm daily.

Next to the Garden of Ruins is the **Bishop's Palace** (Püspöki palota), built at the end of the 18th century. In its library are thousands of ancient volumes, including very important historical and religious texts. The building stones for the palace, incidentally, were taken in part from the ruins of the royal basilica. Opposite the Bishop's Palace is the **Franciscan Church** (Ferencés Templom), built in Baroque style. Open 7-

11:30am. The adjacent **St. Anne's Church** (Szt. Anna Kápolna) was built in 1470 in the Gothic style.

Continue south on Március 15 utca to the King Stephen Museum (István Király Múzeum), at 3 Gagarin tér. On the way, at No. 5, you will pass the **Black Eagle Pharmacy** (Fekete Sas, Patika Múzeum), marked by its Rococo style (1758); and also the **Jesuit Church** next to the **Monastery** (Nos. 6 and 8), both of which were built in the 18th century. In the interesting **King Stephen Museum**, (open Tues.-Sun. 10am-6pm) are archeological artifacts from the Celtic period, as well as ethnographic exhibitions of life in the region.

Bory Vár Castle, the work of the sculptor Bory Jenő, was built in an astonishing mixture of styles: Scottish castle, Gothic fortress, Baroque palace, etc. The figure of Ilona, the wife of the sculptor, is immortalized here in many paintings and sculptures. Open Mar.-Dec. from 9am-5pm. It can be reached on foot or by bus from Marx Square to Mariavolgyi utca, north of the center of town.

Trips outside the city

Lake Velence (Velencei-Tó), a few kms east of the city, offers opportunities for sailing, fishing, and vacationing which have given it the nickname of "Mini-Balaton." One can also visit **Zichy Castle**, built in 1725 in Varpalota, 22 kms west of the city, on road 8 to Veszprém.

Veszprém

Veszprém is the capital of the Bakony region. On most of the hilltops in the city and around it you will find the ruins of castles and fortresses which were built throughout history. Remains were even found of a large settlement from the Stone Age. As far back as the days of King Stephen, the city was an important religious center, and the cathedral, built in the 11th century, was the seat of the local bishopric. Settlement and expansion of the city continued and, today, it has over 200 historical houses built in different styles. Over 60,000 people live in Veszprém, which now serves as an industrial center as well as a center for chemical research.

The city lies on five hills and the valleys between them. Szabadság tér is the heart of the city, and from here, Rákóczi utca continues up Castle Hill (Várhegy). This is the most interesting area in the city, and since the sites are very near to each other, it makes for a pleasant walk.

Veszprém — The Castle

How to get there

Vezprém is located on road E66 which you can join from Szombathely (see the end of the route "Northern Transdanubia") or from Székesfehérv r. The city is on road 73, 16 kms from the vacation town of Csopak on the northern shore of Lake Balaton.

The train which leaves from Déli railroad station in Budapest reaches Veszprém two hours later. The train trip from Székesfehérvár (leaving every hour) takes only 40 minutes. The railway station is quite far away, north of the center of town. To go from it to the center, take a bus down Felszabadulás utca. The bus station is close to the center, a short walk if you go via the market and Ferenc Square.

Tourist services

The efficient *Balaton Tourist* is located at 3 Münnich Ferenc tér (tel. 13-750), and next to it is the *Budapest Tourist*, at No. 2 of

In the city castle

the square (tel. 21-030). A branch of the *IBUSZ* (tel. 12-245) and *Express* (tel. 12-173) are both located at 6 Kossuth Lajos utca.

Food and lodging

The only hotel in the city, *Veszprém* (6 Budapesti utca, tel. 12-345), is a dependable, moderately priced hotel, well located. Lower priced rooms can be found in private homes or at the motel *Erdei Udülőházak*, which rents bungalows outside the city (14 Kittenberger K. utca, tel. 11-971).

The city's restaurants are not particulary good, but you can get international cuisine at *Magyaros* (6 Kossuth Lajos utca) which serves the tourist trade.

What to see

From Rákóczi tér, take a pleasant short walk along Kossuth utca, leading out of the city's new commercial center to Szabadság tér where the **City Hall** is located.

From this square, continue on to Vörös Hadsereg (Red Army) tér. At No. 3 is a **fire lookout tower** (Tűztorony) which, like the one in Sopron, was built and renovated many times, in different styles, starting in the Middle Ages. Climb up for a lovely view of the Bakony Mountains. Open Tues.-Sun. 10am-6pm).

Continue on to the castle district via **Heroes' Gate** (Hősök Kapuja), built during the 30's, using stones taken from the original gate of the citadel. Walk along the narrow street which goes through the castle quarter, until **Bishop's Palace** (Püspöki Palota), built between 1765-1776 by the architect Fellner Jakab with stones from the royal palace. Today, the palace serves as a **Museum of Religious Art**, and has quite a good collection of prayer books and Christian religious objects. In summer, it is open every day from 9am-5pm. At the end of the street is a balcony with a good view of the town and its surroundings.

In the center of the castle district is the **Cathedral**, which was originally built during the first years of the Magyar presence. It has been renovated a few times, finally acquiring a neo-Romanesque facade (12th century). Between the Bishop's Palace and the cathedral is the Gothic style **Gizella Church** (Gizella Kápolna), whose wall paintings are from the 13th century. According to Hungarian tradition, Gizella, the wife of Stephen I, was crowned here as Queen of Hungary. On the other side of the cathedral, are the remains of **St. George Church** (Szt. György Kápolna) from the 10th century, which was uncovered in archeological excavations.

On the way back, behind Heroes' Gate, is the interesting **Castle Museum** (Vármúzeum), devoted to the history of the city and the fortress. This colorful museum sheds light on the history of the area (open during the tourist season Tues.-Sun. from 9am-5pm).

Special events

As part of the **Musical Court Festival**, concerts are held in the castle during July and August. At the beginning of August, potters assemble for a fair where their wares are exhibited and sold.

The Bakony Mountain Range

Sixteen kilometers west of Veszprém, on road 8 is the town of

Herend, with its famous porcelain factory, built in 1839. The **Porcelain Museum** (Porcelán Múzeum) there is open 8:30am-4pm all year; between April and September it is closed on Mondays; from October to March it is closed Fridays. The museum has on display beautiful pieces of porcelains and provides explanations about the manufacturing processes.

Those wanting to get to the heart of the mountain range should continue to the village of Nagyvázsony, 23 kms southwest of Veszprém. Near this small village (1,800 inhabitants) is the **Castle of Kinizsi Pál**, (died 1494) whose statue stands at the entrance to the castle. Kinizsi was a gigantic man, who became a legendary figure as an officer in the army of King Matthias Corvinus. Among his exploits, it is recounted that he used the limbs of a Turkish soldier whom he had killed in order to slay an additional hundred soldiers, and that he celebrated his victory over the Ottoman military unit with a "dance of the three Turks," grabbing one Turk in each hand and grasping the third between his teeth. The castle and the remains of the red marble burial vault are on the slope beneath the village (open daily from 8am-5pm).

From the castle, continue west to the town of **Sümeg**. A fine **medieval castle** (Sümeg Vár) stands proudly on the top of the hill, overlooking the entire area. It is well-preserved, and those wings which have been damaged are undergoing renovation. The castle was built during the 13th century. Fortified with massive walls, it repelled the Turks but fell to the Hapsburgs at the beginning of the 18th century. Below the fortress is a parking lot. From here, you have to climb up on foot — about a fifteen minute walk (closed November-March).

In Sümeg you can see attractive wall paintings in the church (Plébánia Templom), which was built in Baroque style in 1756.

From Sümeg, there is an excellent road south, road 84, which extends to **Szigliget**, 42 kms away, on the shores of the Balaton (see "Lake Balaton").

Lake Balaton

Lake Balaton is the largest lake in central Europe. It covers an area of 600 square kilometers — it is 78 kilometers long and up to 15 kilometers wide. The Hungarians have developed its shores for the vacation industry, which attracts both Hungarians and foreign tourists.

Lake Balaton is a "young" lake that was formed about 20,000 years ago. It is very shallow: its average depth is about three meters. Its name comes from the Slavic word *bolatin* which

Sűmeg

means muddy. The waters of the lake contain minerals such as calcium and magnesium. They were already utilized during Roman times, when medicinal baths were built here. The average temperature of the water during the summer is 22°Celsius.

The southern shore is quite flat and sandy in contrast with the narrow northern shore, which is encircled by a chain of rocky mountains and hills. The southern shore is more suitable for vacationing and for swimming, whereas the northern shore excels in its unique landscapes and natural scenic beauty.

Accommodation on the shores of the Balaton

Many hotels are located at vacation spots along the shores of the lake. In the main tourist centers there are concentrations of good 3-star hotels, offering all the tourist services suitable for a vacation in the sun.

There are more modest hotels in almost every town along the shore. Most tourists stay in guest houses and private rooms, which should be reserved several months in advance. Numerous campsites of varying quality are also found along the shore.

When to come

In winter, Lake Balaton sometimes freezes over for short periods of time. When this happens, a wide variety of winter activities are possible, such as iceskating. However, at that time of the year, the vacation spots are quiet; most are closed. The most ideal weather is from the beginning of June until August. During this season, the area is inundated with tourists, and traffic is heavy. Prices are also at their highest, and it is recommended to reserve a place well in advance. It is quieter along the lake from mid-May to the beginning of June and from mid-August until mid-September, when weather is suitable for vacation: about 18-20°Celsius.

Special Warning! Sudden storms sometimes arise over the lake, causing high waves. If a sudden storm approaches, a yellow flare is shot skyward over the lake, warning all boaters to return to the shore. A red rocket means that the wind velocity has passed the 55 kms per hour limit, and all swimmers must come out of the water.

The northern shore

There are many roads descending from the Bakony Mountains to the northern shore of Lake Balaton. The best route is road 73, from Veszprém which winds through wooded areas and orchards for 16 kms to the village of **Csopak**. This pleasant village is located in a lovely valley of farmland where there are ruins of a medieval church (19 Kossuth Lajos utca). From Csopak, continue about 5 kms on road 71 along the lake shore, until you reach Balatonfüred.

Balatonfüred

The spa town of Balatonfüred has been an important vacation and health resort since the 18th century. The water is thought to possess considerable therapeutic qualities, due to its mineral content. One of the many patients treated here was the Indian poet-author and artist, Rabindranath Tagore, and a boulevard is named after him in the center of town.

How to get there

By train: Many trains leave each day from Déli railroad station in Budapest for the 2.5 hour trip to Balatonfüred. The local train station is northwest of the center of town.

By bus: In addition to the busses which leave from Budapest, busses also come from Veszprém and Nagyvázsony in the Bakony Mountains. Busses leave frequently for the Tihany Peninsula from the central station, next to the railroad station.

By ferry: A ferry connects Balatonfüred with Siófok on the opposite shore and with other destinations on the northern shore.

Tourist services

Balatontourist-Nord is at 5 Blaha-Lujza (tel. 40-281), with an additional branch in the railroad station. The *IBUSZ* office is located at 4a Petőfi Sándor u. (tel. 40-028).

Food and lodging

The *Margaréta* hotel (29 Széchenyi utca, tel. 43-824) is considered the best hotel in town, and is open all year round to serve tourists who come to the medicinal baths. The fine *Eden* hotel (4 Szabadság utca, tel. 42-111) is also open all year.

During the summer two other good hotels are open: the *Annabella* (25 Beloiannisz utca, tel. 42-225) and the modern *Marina* (tel. 43-644), next to the Margareta. The focus for yachting, sailboat, and other water sport enthusiasts is at the Marina.

Aranycsillag (1 Zsigmond utca, tel. 43-466), is simple, clean and comfortable.

Good restaurants are found in the large hotels. Other recommended restaurants are: *Halászkert* at 2 Petőfi Sándor utca and the *Etelbár* bistro at 22 Jókai Mór utca.

What to do

Other than the treatments and bathing, the town does not have many tourist attractions. In the central square, Gyögy tér, are the hospital and a pagoda-like structure. In this building you will find drinking fountains with natural mineral water from the Kossuth springs. It is not very pleasant tasting but is supposed to be good for the heart and the nerves.

In 1926, Tagore planted a tree of remembrance in the memorial grove in the municipal park, where trees had been planted by the Italian winner of the Nobel Prize for Literature, Quasimodo, and other personalities. Another celebrity who lived in the city was the 19th century Hungarian author Jókai Mór. His home has become a memorial museum (1 Honvéd utca, open during winter daily from 10am-6pm. During the rest of the year, closed on Mondays).

Tihany Peninsula

This small peninsula is about 10 kms west of Balatonfüred and can be reached by bus or by ferry. The rocky peninsula, which is a national park, was formed by the extension of the volcanic hills into the lake. You can enjoy a hike of several hours on one of the footpaths which crisscross the peninsula in all directions.

The **Benedictine Monastery** stands at the top of the hill, in the center of the village. The structure was first built in the 11th century under the patronage of King Andrew I, who is buried in the monastery church. Documents pertaining to the construction of this monastery can be found in the Pannonhalma Monastery. In these documents Hungarian words appear in the Latin text, for the first time. A castle was built in the 13th century, surrounding the monastery and the church, but both were destroyed in the course of the wars against the Turks and the Austrians. The church was rebuilt on the ruins of its predecessor in the middle of the 18th century, in Baroque style. The crypt in the church cellar, where King Andrew is buried, still retains its Romanesque character.

In the Benedictine Monastery, where concerts take place in summer, we find the **Tihanyi Museum**, with a lovely view from the eastern windows. This interesting museum contains an exhibition of pictures of Lake Balaton from different periods, Roman relics found in the area, and an impressive exhibit of authentic musical instruments. The museum is open Tues.-Sun. from 10am-6pm.

The small **inner lake** (Belső Tó) is a very tranquil place, and boasts a wealth of greenery. Many fishermen frequent its shores and try to catch carp, octopus, and other creatures. A number of footpaths have been laid out for visitors to the peninsula, including a walk of about an hour from the inner port to the Russian Well (Oroszkút) and to the cells of the monks which were carved out of the basalt rock. This recommended route is marked with green trail signs. Another interesting route, marked in red, leads from the port to the summit of the Csúcs hegy at a height of 235 meters through lush vegetation.

The Tihany Peninsula is considered to be the most beautiful spot on the lake front and is very popular with tourists. The great demand causes crowding and higher prices and, as a result, sometimes it is very difficult to find lodging in the area. It is preferable to continue on and find accommodation somewhere else along the shore. The local tourist bureau *Balaton Tourist-Nord* (20 Kossuth Lajos utca, tel. 44-052) is open from mid-April to the end of September.

Balatonudvari

A small resort, 3 kms west of Tihany, offers a quiet vacation in one of the summer houses along the lake. Several hikes begin in the village, and the trails are well marked in different colors. One of these is the green route, a three-hour hike to the summit of **Cold Mountain** (Hideg hegy), 400 meters high, from which there is a splendid view. For more details and to reserve rooms, contact the tourist bureau in Tihany during the tourist season.

Badacsony

The volcanic mountains of Badacsony boast impressive basalt columns and a massive naturally formed stone gate, a counterpoint to the tranquility of the calm lake.

In the *Balatontourist-Nord* tourist bureau (10 Park utca, tel. 149) you can organize jeep trips to the **Stone Gate Cliffs** (Kőkapu Sziklái). You can also reach them by taking a pleasant hike, on the trail marked in red, starting at the local railway station, via a church made out of basalt stone and the Monastery Well springs (Klastromkút Forrás).

Badacsony is known throughout Europe for its excellent wine. The combination of the hillsides of volcanic soil and the proper amount of sun not only smiles upon the vineyards but also warms the heart. The **Wine Museum**, open from 3pm-5pm (Fő Ut) and the **Wine-tasting Bar** (Borkóstoló) in the next village, **Badacsonytomaj**, attract more tourists than the **Literary Museum** (Irodalmi Emlékmúzeum). This museum was opened in the home of Roza Szegedi, wife of the poet and author Kisfaludy Sándor, whose possessions and furniture are exhibited here (open during the tourist season Tues.-Sun. from 10am-6pm).

Keszthely — Festetics Palace

You may want to continue on for a view of the **Rózsakő**, a volcanic slab. Legend has it that if you sit on it with your back to the Balaton and think of your loved one, you will marry her (or him) during that same year.

Szigliget

This delightful farm village, whose houses have sloped thatched roofs, nestles between two hilltops which rise up north of Balaton. At the foot of the northern hill stands a lovely village church, from which a trail climbs to the top of the hill. On the hilltop are the remains of **Szigliget Castle**. This ancient castle was built in the 13th century and heroically withstood the Turkish invaders. The Austrian Hapsburgs destroyed it, and today only the ruins of some of the walls remain.

Keszthely

Keszthely is the largest town along the shore, and it has about 24,000 inhabitants. It is considered to be one of the most attractive and pleasant places on the lake front. The town is active all year round as a commercial and cultural center, unlike most of the resorts on the lake shore. In the past, from the beginning of the 18th century until the end of the Second World War, the town was almost completely owned by the Festetics family, of the Hungarian aristocracy.

Festetics Palace which is in the town is thought to be one of the most beautiful palaces in the country. When you are there you can arrange a trip to the famous Hévíz baths (7 kms west of the city; see special appendix on spas in Hungary).

How to get there

By train: From the Déli railroad station in Budapest take the express train to the southern shore, change to the local train at Balaton Szentgyörgy, and then circle around the lake from the southwest. The train station is located within walking distance of the main square (Fő tér).

Busses: It is easy to reach Keszthely by bus from places on the northern shore such as Badacsony. Busses arrive hourly from Szombathely. The bus station is located next to the train station.

By ferry: From the dock at Keszthely, boats leave for the nearby harbor at Balatongyörök (a 40 minute trip) and Siófok.

Tourist services

Zalatour is located at 1 Fő tér (tel. 12-560). *IBUSZ* bureau is at 1 Széchenyi (tel. 12-951), and those needing the services of the *Express* agency will find it at 22 Kossuth utca (tel. 12-032).

Food and lodging

Hotel *Helikon* (tel. 11-330), located on the lake shore, is the best in town and one of the most pleasant along the shores of Balaton. At *Amazon* (11 Szabadság út, tel. 12-448) the rooms are clean and inexpensive. On the hilly shore, are several campsites with bungalows and suitable places to set up tents and caravans.

The place to eat here is in one of the restaurants on Kossuth Lajos utca. Among the best, we recommend the garden of the *Hungária* (35 Kossuth Lajos utca) and the excellent *Béke* at No. 50 of the same street, where the food is served to the accompaniment of Gypsy music.

What to see

The **Balaton Museum** (2 Múzeum utca) is open in summer

Tues.-Sun. from 10am-6pm, and during the rest of the year from 9am-5pm. Here we find archeological artifacts from the 1st century AD onward, as well as an interesting ethnographic exhibition. From the museum, Kossuth utca leads to Fő tér in the center of the city. There you will find the 14th century Gothic **Church** and the **City Hall**, built in Louis XVI style at the end of the 18th century. Continue walking up the street to reach the main tourist attraction in town — the palace of Count Festetics.

Festetics Palace (Festetics Kastély) was constructed over a period of 150 years, starting in 1745. It contains a chapel, a concert hall, and an archive, in addition to luxurious living quarters and guest rooms. Special notice should be taken of the rich library with its wooden shelves and ceiling candelabra,which contains more than 50,000 volumes. All of the fashionable Hungarian writers and poets of the 19th century were invited to the palace for parties and literary discussions. Open Tues.-Sun. from 10am-6pm. Visitors must put cloth overshoes over their footwear, in order to protect the delicate wooden floor.

After the visit to the palace, you can continue up Georgikon Street to the **Agricultural College**, the first in Europe, built by the dynamic Count György Festetics in 1797. In summer, the Agricultural College's historical museum at 67 Bercsényi utca is open every day between 10am-5pm

The Southern Shore

Siófok

Siófok, 106 kms southwest of Budapest, is the major resort town on the shores of Lake Balaton. Until 1861, it was unknown, but when railroad tracks connected Siófok to other parts of the country the place became a desirable vacation spot for the more prosperous citizens of Hungary. Today, the town boasts the biggest well-tended bathing beach on the lake — 15 kms long. 22,000 people live in the town.

How to get there

By train: Trains leave every hour from Déli railroad station in Budapest, for the two hour journey to Siófok. International trains leave from Siófok every day on their way to Yugoslavia (Zagreb). Those wanting to go to Austria (Vienna) need to change trains at Székesfehérvar. The local train station in Siófok is next to Szabadság Square, walking distance, via Kinizsi Pál Street, from the beach and from the tourist sites.

By bus: There is a good bus connection to Budapest, Austria (Vienna) and Czechoslovakia (Bratislava). The bus station is next to the train station.

SIÓFOK

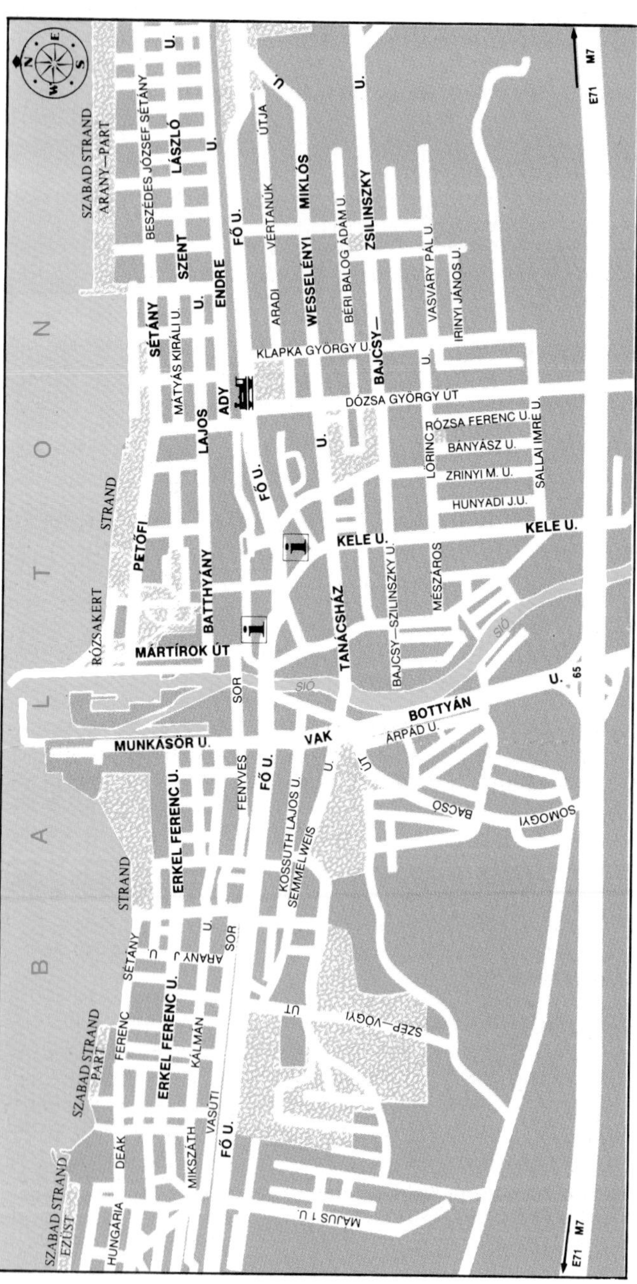

By ferry: Siófok is a center for ferry boat sailings. The most popular lines from Siófok include the sailings to Balatonfüred (50 minutes), Tihany (40 minutes), and a trip along the shore to Keszthely, which includes most of the beaches at the lake and takes about six hours.

Tourist services

The main office of the *Siótour* is located near the train and bus stations (6 Szabadság tér, tel. 10-900). This agency has additional offices, including an efficient branch at 13 Petőfi sétány (Hotel *Hungaria*). *IBUSZ* is at 174 Fő utca (tel. 11-107).

Food and lodging

The best hotels in Siófok are located all along Petőfi Sandor Blvd., near the lake shore. Most of them have good restaurants, a private beach, money-changing services, etc. The price for a double room is about $50 a night, for bed and breakfast. All the hotels open on May 1 and operate until October 15.

Balaton (9 Petőfi S. Sétány, tel. 10-655) is the first hotel at the beginning of the row, and next to it are the *Lido* (at No. 11, tel. 10-633), the *Hungaria* (at No. 13, tel. 10-677), and the *Europa* (at No. 15, tel. 13-411). These hotels are very similar in quality and services offered, and reservations may be made at any of them by telexing 22-4108 and indicating the name of the hotel you prefer.

For less crowded and expensive accommodation, try *Napfény* (8 Mártirok utca, tel. 11-408) in the municipal park. Those arriving off season will need accommodations in one of the simple hostels, such as the pension *Csiba* at 8 Kiss utca, west of the city center.

The good restaurants in the city are found near the best hotels: *Siófok* restaurant, next to *Európa* hotel, is considered one of the best in town, as is *Csárdás* restaurant (105 Fő utca). In all the good restaurants, international cuisine is served along with Hungarian dishes.

What to see

Those interested in some historical information about the city can visit **Beszédes József Múzeum**, 2 Sió utca (open from mid-May to the end of October Tues.-Sun., 9am-1pm and 2pm-6pm; from November to mid-May 9am-1pm), located near the bridge on the Sió, west of Szabadság tér. The museum focuses on the water supply of the Danube and of Lake Balaton, and it also has a conventional ethnographic exhibit. Near the museum is the colorful covered market. In the city's cultural center, at

Fő tér (tel. 10-072) a variety of programs are performed. For details, contact the tourist bureaus and the large hotels.

The **nightclubs** in the city try to attract the vacationers with programs brought from Budapest. Among the nightclubs, are: *Mayin* at 14 Batthyány utca, *Eden*, at 15 Potőfi sétány (*Hotel Europa*), and *Pipacs* at 11 Mártirok utca.

Zamárdi

This village, 9 kms west of Siófok, has a long history. It is mentioned in documents from as early as 1082. In addition to sunbathing, you can visit a Baroque church, built in 1774 and see a typical village house on the main street, Fő utca. Today, 3,000 people live in the town, and there is a railway station. Because the lake is so shallow here, the water warms up very quickly. The *Siótour* tourist agency operates an office here (12 Kossuth utca, tel. 31-072).

Szántod

Four kms west of Zamárdi, Szántod is located at the narrow part of the lake and is only 1.5 kms from the Tihany Peninsula on the other side of the lake. Ferries leave every 20 minutes from Szántod Rév for the ten minute trip to the northern shore. In June-August, the ferry operates from 7am-12:30am. The ferry also has arrangements for car transport.

The **Ferry Inn** (Rév Csárda) was built beside the dock, about 150 years ago, in the Baroque style, and is still very popular with tourists.

Balatonföldvár

The demand for vacation spots on the shores of the Balaton at the end of the 19th century resulted in the creation of a new resort, which was built especially for the Hungarian aristocracy. It was built 14 kms from Siófok with the support of the family of the famous Count Széchenyi. Even though the place is used only for vacationing, it has retained a pleasant, friendly atmosphere. Because of its informality, single men and women gather here in order to sunbathe by day and circulate among the restaurants and bars at night. The town has a well-tended beach, a pleasant boardwalk, and a small port.

The train station is located at the entrance to the resort, a little east of the center of town. *Siótour* is at 9-11 Hősök utca (tel. 40-099); *IBUSZ* — 14 Balatonszentgyörgyi utca (tel. 40-066); *Express* — 9 József A. utca (tel. 40-313).

This is the starting point of a popular trip to the village of **Kőröshegy**, 3 kms to the south. It has a well preserved Gothic church from the 15th century in which classical concerts take place during the summer season. You can reach the village by local bus from the center of the resort.

Balatonszárszó

This small village, with 2,000 inhabitants, 6 kms from Balatonföldvár, is famous because of the proletarian poet József Attila who threw himself under the wheels of a train here and died in 1937 at the age of 32. The house where he lived is now a small museum which was established to honor his memory (7 József Attila utca). The village is one of the quietest spots along the shore, and is an ideal place for those seeking an intimate and quiet vacation. *Siótour* office is in the center of town next to the train station (tel. 40-456).

Balatonszemes

Five kms further is the village of Balatonszemes. The **Owl Castle** (Bagolyvár) was built on the ruins of the Clown Tower (Bolondvár), which was destroyed at the end of the Turkish occupation in the 17th century.

Boglárlelle

Boglárlelle combines the two villages of Balatonlelle and Balatonboglr, which became vacation resorts at the end of the last century. Today, this is typical vacation resort and is quite crowded.

The tower on **Castle Hill** (Várhegy) is a splendid observation point. There is a local art exhibit during the summer season in Temetőhegy. Programs of folkdancing for tourists are held in the **Cultural Center** (2 Kossuth Lajos utca), which was built in the middle of the last century in neo-Classical style. Here, the annual convention of woodworkers in Hungary is held, and there is an exhibit of their work.

The *Siótour* tourist agency has offices in Balatonboglár (3 Dozsa György utca, tel. 50-665), and in Balatonlelle (1 Szt. István utca).

Fonyód

The resort town of Fonyód developed at the foot of the volcanic hills (Fonyód hegy), 45 kms west of Siófok. A church, built here in the Middle Ages, became a fortified castle with the approach of the Turkish invaders. In the 15th century, after the Turkish conquest, the place was destroyed. You can still see its ruins if you climb up to the summit of Castle Hill (it takes about one hour). Starting from the railroad station, the wooded trail is marked in red on the signposts along its route.

There are several small, attractive beaches, including campsites and small guest houses here. *Siótour* office is next to the train station. The boat trip to Badacsony on the opposite shore takes about 45 minutes, and the ferry sails several times a day.

Balatonberény

This is the last in the row of resort towns stretching along the southern shore. It has a Gothic church, built about 500 years ago and renovated in 1733 in the Baroque style. At the nearby nature reserve of Little Balaton Lake (Kis Balaton), there are many varieties of birds who live on the lake and in the surrounding marsh. This visit requires written permission given in advance by the Nature Reserve Authority in Budapest (*Országos Természet-es Környezetvédelmi Hivatal*, 21 Kőltő utca). The *Siotour* office is at 2 Balaton utca.

From here, the road winds down to the lake shore on its way to Keszthely, which was the last place of interest on our tour of the northern side of the lake.

Special events along the lake shore

May: The summer season opens with yacht trips in the last week of May in Balatonfüred.

July: Anna Báll Festival at the end of July in Balatonfüred (programs, dancing, and beauty queen contest).

August: Pottery Fair in Vesprém.

September: Grape Harvesting Festival in Badacsony.

During the summer, many classical music concerts are held, including the excellent concerts in the Festetics Palace in Keszthely. Organ concerts take place in ancient churches in Keszthely, Tihany, etc. Hungarian pop and rock groups perform in the squares and public parks. For details, contact the tourist bureaus.

South Transdanubia

Pécs

Pécs is the most important city in the southern part of Hungary, with about 180,000 inhabitants. It is located at the foot of the Mecsek mountain range, whose summits reach a height of 600 meters. There are coal and uranium mines in the mountains. The city is surrounded by wide areas of farm land, including many orchards and vineyards, which have given the area a reputation for its excellent fruits and wines. The Turkish traveller Evliya Çelebi, who was a guest of the governor of the city during the Turkish occupation in the 17th century, tells of 42 different kinds of pears which he ate during his visit to the city! The climate is very pleasant, and the museums are as numerous and as varied as the afore mentioned pears.

History of the city

The temperate climate of Pécs and its location between the Mecsek mountains and the plains below attracted settlers to the region beginning from the Neolithic period.

The Romans arrived in the area near the beginning of the Christian Era and developed the city because of its strategic importance in controlling the lowlands in the area. In the 3rd century, the city was proclaimed the capital of the Roman province of Valeria. Dissolution of the Roman Empire brought the decline of the city and the loss of its wealth, and most of its inhabitants abandoned it. Only a small settlement remained until the Magyar conquest in the 10th century AD.

King Stephen gave the city a new thrust, when, in 1009, he established the bishopric here, and built the cathedral on the ruins of a large Roman structure. In the Middle Ages, Pécs was one of the most important religious and cultural centers in Hungary. The first university in the country was established here in 1367.

The Turkish conquest in 1543, after the Hungarian defeat at the battle of Mohács (30 kms to the east), left Pécs without much resistance. The Turkish occupation, which lasted about 150 years, left its mark on the city in the form of splendid mosques and other public buildings. Many of them were destroyed in 1686, after heavy battles that forced the Turks out by the Holy

League. This was an alliance formed by Pope Innocent VI against the Turks, which included the Hapsburg Empire and its supporters, Poland and Venice. During the 18th and 19th centuries, the city was rebuilt. Most of its buildings were restored in the style of the period, and they give the center of the city its unique character and appearance.

Geographical location

You can reach Széchenyi tér, the center of the city, via taxi or bus No. 30 from the train station. Most of the interesting sites are within a short walking distance of the square. This is the site of the old city, still enclosed by the ruins of a wall on its northern side.

The old city is surrounded by residential neighborhoods and industrial areas on three sides and by the Mecsek hills on the north. The houses of the city extend over the northern hill, where some hotels are also located.

How to get there

By train: Several direct trains connect the southern and eastern railroad stations of Budapest to Pécs. The trip takes about 3 hours. Those coming from Lake Balaton leave from Siófok; those coming from Zagreb in Yugoslavia stop at the Hungarian border town of Gyékényes and continue on to Pécs via the slow local train (three hours).

By bus: The *Volan* company operates a direct bus between Budapest and Pécs daily. The trip takes about three hours. Other busses come from Héviz, Szeged and Veszprém. Travellers coming from Yugoslavia by bus can use the direct line from the Yugoslavian city of Osijek.

By car: The good road, 6 (E73), connects Budapest to Pécs, a distance of about 200 kms. From Yugoslavia it is best to come from Osijek (96 kms to the south) or from Zagreb (230 kms southwest of Pécs).

Tourist services

The municipal tourist office, *Mecsek Tourist* (tel. 14-866) and *IBUSZ* (tel. 12-148) are located next to each other in Széchenyi tér. Foreign currency can also be changed here. They are open from 8:30am-4pm. *Express* is located at 6 Bajcsy-Zsilinszky utca (tel.12-793), opposite the central bus station and the marketplace.

The post office is at the intersection of Jókay Mór and Rákóczi Streets.

Food and lodging

Palatinus hotel (5 Kossuth L. utca, tel. 33-022), the best in town, is rather expensive. The building, as well as the lobby, are designed in the classic style. The modern and comfortable *Pannonia* is located opposite the Hassan Yakovali Mosque (3 Rácókzi utca, tel. 13-332). *Főnix* (2 Hunyadi út, tel. 11-680) has showers adjoining most of the rooms, but a common toilet on the first floor only, for all the rooms.

Fenyves (64 Szőlő utca, tel. 15-996) is highly recommended and offers a veranda overlooking the city. *Hunyor* (16 Jurisics M. utca, tel. 15-677), which is more expensive, was built as a comfortable vacation hotel, even though it is all cement and concrete. Both are in the northern suburbs of the Meczek hills.

As in all Hungarian cities, here too, you can find less expensive accommodation in private rooms.

Good restaurants are found in the city's hotels. Next to Széchenyi tér you can eat at *Dóm Vendéglő* in the shopping mall (3 Kossuth Lajos utca). In this restaurant, favored by Hungarians as well as tourists. There is a wooden replica of the Pécs cathedral. The menus are in English, German, and French and there is pop background music.

What to see

A suitable starting point for a tour of the city is Széchenyi tér. In the square is the **Turkish Mosque**, largest in the country, called Gázi Kászim Pasa Dzsámija. It was built in the second half of the 16th century, at the site of an ancient church. In the large mosque, used now as a church, it is still possible to distinguish the Seljuk calligraphy in the corner of the prayer niche. Behind the mosque, at house No. 12, is an archeological exhibition, part of the **Janus Pannonius Museum**. The man after whom the museum was named was a bishop in the 15th century and was a renowned philosopher, poet, and a great philanthropist. Relics found in the region from the prehistoric period until the Magyar conquest are exhibited in the building, erected in the 17th century. This museum is quite interesting and is open Tues.-Sun. from 10am-4pm.

We turn west on Janus Pannonius utca to the **Csontváry Museum** at Nos. 11-13, devoted to the paintings of the Hungarian artist Csontváry Kosztka Tivadar (1853-1919). In his works, large oil paintings, Csontváry immortalized places and events from his travels throughout Europe and the Near East, using strong exciting colors (some of which are also exhibited in the National Gallery in Budapest). This talented artist ended his life in an institution for the mentally ill. The museum is open Tues.-Sun. from 10am-4pm.

SOUTH TRANSDANUBIA

A few steps from the Csontváry Museum is lovely Dóm tér, in which we find the famous Cathedral of Pécs.

The **Cathedral** (Székesegyház) was built in the 11th century, probably on ancient Roman ruins. It was destroyed and has been rebuilt several times since then. The impressive structure we see today was completed in 1891. On the facade of the cathedral eleven arches were built, and on top of them, marble statues of the twelve apostles look out over the square. Inside, the cathedral is adorned with paintings and black marble columns, which surround the altar. Open Tues.-Sun. from 9am-1pm and 2-6pm. To the west, in a lovely park, is a small, circular, crenellated bastion. This is the **Barbakán**, built in the 15th century on the walls of the city as a forward defense position against the Turkish invader. It was restored during the 1960's.

East of the cathedral, at 6 Káptalan utca is a museum with

Pécs — The main square

The cathedral of Pécs

the works of Martin Ferenc on exhibit (open Tues.-Sun. from 10am-2pm)

Further up Káptalan Street, in building No. 3, is a small but excellent museum of modern art in the house of the famous painter **Victor Vásárely**. The painter, who was born in Pécs as Vásárdhelyi Győző, was one of the first proponents of *Op Art*. On the first floor are works of several modern artists, including his wife Claire, and his son Jean-Pierre Yvaral. The second floor is devoted entirely to his works — sculpture-paintings which achieve their effect from the interplay of color and form. The museum is open Tues.-Sun. from 10am-4pm.

The **Zsolnay Porcelain Museum** (2 Káptalan utca) is located in the oldest building in Pécs. The building was erected in the first half of the 14th century and it holds an impressive collection of famous hand-painted porcelain vessels produced in the city since 1852. From the Zsolnay Museum, we take Leonardo da Vinci Street back to Széchenyi tér.

Take Bajcsy-Zsilinszky utca to the **Great Synagogue** (5 Kossuth tér), which was built between 1865-1869 in Romanesque style. Eversince the Pécs Jewish community was destroyed, the synagogue has served as a museum. Open from May 1 until mid-October, Sun.-Fri. 9am-1pm and 1;30pm-7pm.

The subterranean **Fish and Reptile Zoo** (Akvárium-Terrárium), 31 Munk csy Mihály utca, (between the shopping mall and the Synagogue) contains a collection of reptiles, including pythons, iguanas, and alligators, as well as a collection of fish (open from 10am-5pm).

Two more sites from the Turkish period are the **Jakovali Hassan Pasa Mosque** (2 Rákócszi utca), opposite *Hotel Pannonia* (open all week except Wednesdays, from 10am-6pm); and the **Mausoleum of Idris Baba** (Idrisz baba Türbéje) at 8 Nyár Street.

Shopping

Shopping enthusiasts can enjoy wandering around Kossuth Lajos mall which starts at Széchenyi tér, or Sallai utca which is on the other side of the square.

Porcelain objects from the *Zsolnay* factory, may be bought at the factory shop (2 Jókay tér). The vegetable and fruit market is next to the central bus station and is better suited for "candid" photos than for shopping purposes.

Special events

Organ recitals take place in spring and summer in the beautiful cathedral. Less interesting for tourists is the Hungarian Drama Festival which takes place here during June and July.

Excursions from Pécs

The resort towns of **Orfű** and **Abaliget**, about 20 kms northeast of Pécs in the western part of the Mecsek, attract those tourists who want to flee from the city heat and the crowds during the height of the tourist season. In Abaliget there is a stalactite and stalagmite cave with a stream running through it. Orfű is located near lakes where you can swim, sail, or fish. Rooms in private homes or in small guest houses can be reserved between May and September at the branch office of the *Mecsek Tourist*, located at the campsite near Abaliget (tel. 78-070). Out of season, the tourist bureau moves to 1 Széchenyi Square in Abaliget (tel. 78-028).

Thirty three kms west of Pécs, on road 6 which leads to the Yugoslavian border, is the **Island Castle** (Szigetvár). It was built at the end of the 14th century on an island in the Almás Patak River which flows through the town. This castle had its hour of glory in the summer of 1566, when 90,000 Turkish soldiers under the command of sultan Suleiman the Great attacked it. About 2,000 defenders, led by Zrinyi Miklós, were garrisoned there. The defenders surrendered after a siege lasting 33 days and a desperate battle ensued, causing the Turks heavy losses. The castle, renovated during the 60's, and the Turkish mosque which still stands at Zrinyi tér can be visited, but it is not worth a special trip to this sleepy town. It is of interest primarily for those travelling to Yugoslavia via the border crossing at the town of Barcs, 30 kms west of Szigetvár.

The spa town of **Harkány** is 25 kms south of Pécs on road 58. The spring water here contains sulphur and fluoride at a temperature of 60° Celsius. The town now attracts many who come for medical treatment. Apart from the baths, there is not much to find in Harkány (see more details in the appendix "Medicinal Baths in Hungary"), so most tourists continue east for 6 kms to Siklós.

Siklós

During the Roman period, Siklós was already known as a way station called Seres. Here, interest focuses on the **Siklós Castle** (Siklós Vár), built at the beginning of the 15th century. The present appearance of the fortress is the result of construction undertaken at the beginning of the 18th century and of restoration done between 1954-1969. The castle contains a place of worship, built in the Gothic style, and three floors of historical and artistic exhibits. During the 1960's, when the interior of

PECS

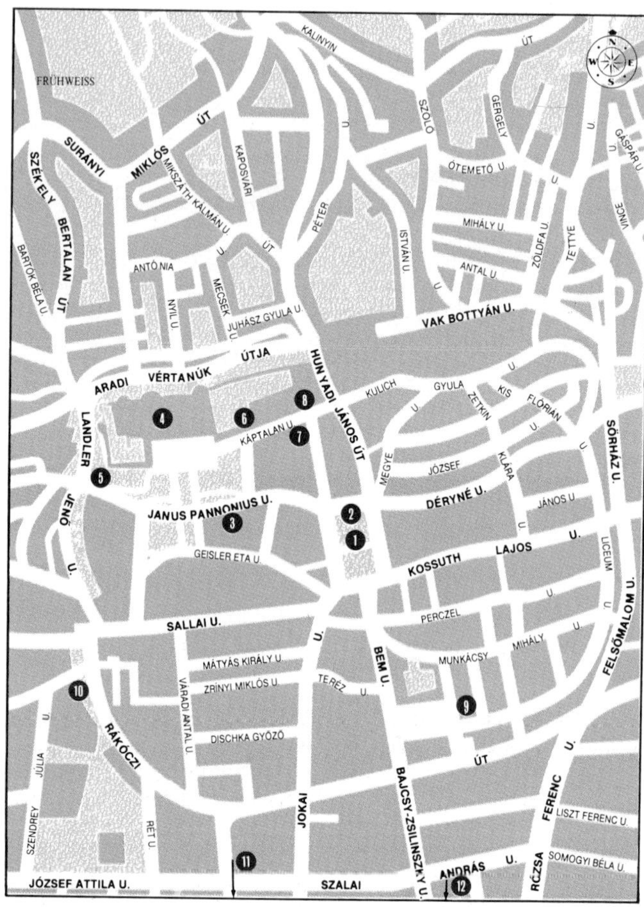

Index

1. Szécheny Square
2. Kászim Pasa Mosque
3. Csontváry Museum
4. The Cathedral
5. The Barbakán Bastion
6. Martin Ferenc Museum
7. Vásárely Museum
8. Porcelain Museum
9. Synagogue
10. Jakovali Mosque
11. To the railway station
12. To the bus station and the farmers' market

In the Csontváry Museum

the castle was renovated, a restaurant, hotel, and hostel were added.

One can continue on beyond Siklós for 13 kms to the east to the winery town of **Villany**. This is a typical vineyard town, where grapes have been pressed by trampling for more than 2,000 years. You can drink (and buy) the excellent local wines.

Mohács

Forty kms east of Pécs, on road 57, is the town of Mohács. On August 29, 1526 two armies met near here in a battle which had a decisive influence on the history of the country. The defenders, led by Hungarian King Louis II, fought the Turkish army led by Suleiman the Great. The Hungarian army was defeated by the Turkish invaders, the king died in battle, and for the next 150 years, Hungary came under Turkish rule. Relics from the battlefield can be found in the Municipal Museum (2 Szerb utca).

The city, located on the bank of the Danube, serves today as a large port for river barges, and is famous for its *Busó* masks. These masks have the faces of creatures which are a combination of animals and humans. The masks and other costume paraphenalia are worn on March 1, when the local people take to the streets, with torches in hand, to celebrate the ancient **Bosójarás Festival**. The purpose of the celebration to welcome the spring season.

The border station to Yugoslavia is at Udvar, 10 kms south of Mohács.

From Pécs to Budapest

The road from Pécs to Budapest is not especially interesting, and most tourists do not stop on the way. Those with time on their hands can visit the town of **Szekszárd**, 54 kms north of Pécs on road 6. Here, grapes have been grown and wine produced since the time of the Romans, when the city was called Alisca. There is an **Archeological Museum** (Béri Balog Adám Múzeum) in Felszabadulás tér.

The town is of interest mostly as the starting point for a trip to the **Gemenc Forest** (Gemenci-erdő), the largest hunting reserve in Hungary, a remnant of the huge forests which were in abundance in Hungary hundreds of years ago. There are hunting areas here and a national nature reserve, which can be visited — but only with a tour organized by the tourist agencies in the town (*Tolna Tourist*, 38 Széchenyi utca, tel. 12-144). The tour includes a boat trip, a ride on the park train, and observation of the animals freely roaming in the park, including deer, wild boar, and a variety of fowl.

Kalocsa

The town of Kalocsa is located on the other side of the Danube. This farm town was built in the 11th century on the bank of the Danube, but a change in the river's course resulted in its now being about six kms east of the river. The town is a center for growing the peppers from which the national red spice, paprika, is made. And indeed the **Paprika Museum** in this town is devoted to that spice, (Paprik s Múzeum, at 6 Marx tér). Open May to October from Tues.-Sun. 10am-6pm.

Kalocsa is the unofficial capital of Hungarian folklore. You can visit the **Kalocsa Folk Art Cooperative** (Kalocsai Népmuʳvészeti Szővetkezet) at 7 Toma utca which has a permanent exhibition of folk handicrafts, such as embroidery and pottery. It is open Tues.-Sun. from 10am-6pm. During the summer season, there are programs of Hungarian folkdances for tourists. For details, contact the local tourist bureau (*Pusztatourist*, 35 Istv n Király utja, tel. 779).

From here, it is about 120 kms to Budapest on road 51. You can drive along this road until Solt and then change to the E73 expressway.

Great Puszta Plains

The great plains in eastern Hungary cover over half the territory of the country — between the Danube (in the west), the Romanian border (in the east), the Russian border (in the northeast) and the mountain ranges of northern Hungary. In the past, this prairie was thickly forested and constituted an ideal hiding place for nomadic tribes and bands of robbers. It was referred to by the Romans as the "land of the Barbarians". The Romans designated the west bank of the river as their border and fortified their cities against the danger of invasion from the wild forested plain. During the Middle Ages, small towns cropped up in the area, controlled by local tribes, surrounded by small farm villages.

After the battle of Mohács in 1526, many of the inhabitants fled from the villages to the cities, and the region again became a dangerous no-man's-land, the domain of robbers and rebels who fought the Turks (*hajduk*). The Ottoman conquerors made military forays into the area to punish the local population and to chop down trees for military construction. The destruction and ruin in the area earned it the name *Puszta*, meaning destroyed and abandoned. After the Turks were driven out, the area remained desolate and isolated for more than 100 years, due to the difficulty in reaching its marshlands.

The 19th century and the economic growth of Hungary brought resources to this abandoned region and caused its speedy development. The broad plains attracted enterprising farmers and tradesmen as well as romantic writers, artists, and poets, who were enchanted with the wide open spaces and natural beauty of the area. They called the region Alföld, meaning the "Great Plain."

Kecskemét

The first point of interest for tourists coming from Budapest southeast to the Great Plain is the city of Kecskemét. It is reached from Budapest by the train which leaves the western railway station, or by bus from the Népstadion Station. In this city, about 90 kms from Budapest, there are about 100,000 inhabitants, and it is famous chiefly for its apricot orchards

Cifra Palace — Art Nouveau

and the brandy made from them (*barackpalinka*). The city also produces about one third of all the wine in the country.

The heart of the city is the two wide adjacent squares, Szabadság tér and Kossuth tér. In the southeast corner of Kossuth tér is the grand, ornate **Town Hall**. Next to it, three handsome churches were built: to the right of the Town Hall is the **Catholic Church**; opposite it, on the right, the **Franciscan Church**, built in the 18th century and, to the left, in the center of the square, the **Calvinist Church**, built in the 17th century, and covered with climbing vines.

Keckemét

Behind the Calvinist church is a narrow pedestrian mall. The white structure on the right is the **Home of Zoltán Kodály**, the famous musician. It now houses the Music Academy of Kecskemét. It is not open to the public. All along the narrow lane are a number of souvenir shops for tourists.

South of Kossuth tér is the municipal theater, an impressive classical white structure.

Cifra Palace, on the far side of Szabadság tér, at the corner of Rákóczi, was built in the Art Nouveau style. Today, it houses the Municipal Museum, with a selection of art works and exhibits of local history. Among the artists whose works are exhibited here, special mention should be made of Farkas István.

Opposite Cifra Palace, on the other side of Rákóczi Street, stands what used to be a synagogue. Today, this impressive white building serves as a center of science and technology. It can be visited on Saturdays and Sundays, when no other activity is taking place there.

The local **Museum of History** (Katona József Múzeum) is named after the playwright József Katona who was born here (1 Bethlen körút, open Tues.-Sun. 10am-6pm and closed Mondays). Children will be interested in the activities of the **Toy Museum** (Szófkaténusz Játékmühely-és Múzeum) at 1 Gáspár András utca. Open Tues.-Sun. 10am-6pm.

The local tourist bureau is *Pusztatourist* (Szabadság tér, tel. 29-499); *IBUSZ* branch is at 1-3 Széchenyi tér, (tel. 20-557).

Four kms south of Kecskemét is the **Bugac-Puszta National Park**, open Tues.-Sun. from 10am-5pm. The park tries to preserve the atmosphere of the green prairies and has a famous inn built in the old style called *Bugac Csárda*. The park also offers trips on horse back within its boundaries. The park can be reached from Kecskemét by train, bus, or with a trip organized by the tourist agencies in the city. From Bugac, we continue about 60 kms south to Szeged, on the Tisza River.

Szeged

The first settlement here dates from some time during the first thousand years BC, during the period of the Illyrian civilization, but only in the first half of the 13th century AD did it begin to flourish as an agricultural and cultural center. King Béla IV built a castle in the city, which lasted until the Turkish conquest in 1543. The Tisza River flooded the city in March 1879, destroying most of the houses and public buildings. Less than 300 houses remained standing.

During the hundred years since the flood, the city has been repaired and rebuilt. Today, it is a cultural and economic center, with about 180,000 inhabitants and a large university, one of the most important in Hungary.

Szeged is built on the western bank of the Tisza River, similar to the way Pest sits on the Danube: the center of the city, which includes the historical Dóm Square, is the inner core. It is separated from the wide residential boulevards. These boulevards are named after the cities which offered assistance in the reconstruction of the city after the big flood. The Tisza River may be crossed via the bridge which leads from Roosevelt tér in the center of the inner city to the thermal baths on the eastern bank.

How to get there

From Budapest, it is possible to reach Szeged by bus from the

Népstadion station and by train from the western railway station (about 2.5 hours). From the railway station at Baross tér to Dóm tér it is a short walk along Aprilis 4 utca. The central bus station is located at Marx tér, in the western part of the city, between London and Paris Boulevards.

Szeged is close to the Yugoslavian and Romanian borders. Those coming from Romania should travel from the city of Arad via road E68, via the border crossing at Magylak, about 30 kms east of Szeged. Those coming from Yugoslavia should travel from Subotica via road E75 to the border crossing at Hopgos, only 16 kms from Szeged.

Tourist services

Szegedtourist has several offices in the city. The central office is at 7 Klauzál tér (tel. 26-533). *IBUSZ* agency is opposite the local tourist bureau, at No. 2 of the same square (tel. 11-188), and the *Express* agency is located a little west of the square (3 Kigyó utca, tel. 11-310).

Food and lodging

Hungária hotel (2 Komócsin Z. tér, tel. 21-211), the best hotel in town (three stars), is located on the bank of the river, north of the city center. At the hotel you can hire boats for sailing on the river. You can also eat in the fine restaurant there.

Tisza (1 Wesselényi utca, tel. 12-466) and the *Royal* (1 Kölcsey utca, tel. 12-911, telex 82-403) are located in the city center and both are dependable and reasonably priced hotels.

It is possible to find inexpensive rooms in *Móra Fogadó*, an established and quite crowded pension, beside the market at Szt. István tér (36 Bocskai utja, tel. 13-533) or at *Sárkány Fogadó*, opposite the train station (tel. 10-514). Rooms are also available in private homes, beds in student dormitories (via *Express* agency) and camping next to the *Napfény* hotel in Dorozsmai Street, west of the city.

Good restaurants can be found in the central squares, such as the Fish Inn (*Halász-csárda*) at 14 Roosevelt tér, and *Alabárdos* (13 Oskola utca).

What to see

Those walking from the train station along Aprilis 4 utja on the way to Aradi Vértanúk tér, will pass the **Heroes' Gate** (Hősök Kapuja), erected in 1936 by Horthy. From this square, an ornate gate leads to **Church Square** (Dóm tér).

The most impressive landmark in the city is the large **Votive Church** (Fogadalmi Templom), which stands in the center of the square. Its name comes from the vow taken by the city's leading citizens to erect a grand church as a memorial to those who perished in the flood of 1879 and as a symbol of the rebirth of the city. Building began in 1913 and was completed in 1930. The neo-Romanesque church reached a height of 54 meters and its towers extended to a height almost double this. The church facade is embellished with a huge marble statue of the Virgin Mary, three meters high, and a colorful mosaic depicting the twelve apostles. Everything is done on a grand scale. The tremendous organ possesses over nine thousand pipes.While in Szeged on Sunday, don't miss the Mass here.

The **Tower of St. Demetrius** (Szt. Dömötor Torony) in front of the gigantic churchyard overshadowed by it, is one of the oldest buildings in the city. It was built in the 12th century. The **Serbian Church** on the edge of the square was built in the 18th century, and, next to it, a new wing was added which contains the Somogy Library. The large square is the scene for performances of the Summer Theater Festival which takes place between mid-July and mid-August.

Oskola utca leads from the large square north to Roosevelt tér, from which a bridge leads to the thermal baths and the residential quarters in Ujszeged, east of the river. The **Municipal Museum** (Móra Ferenc Múzeum) is at 1 Roosevelt tér, north of the bridge. It is housed in the Palace of Education and Culture built in 1896 in neo-Classical style. Its facade is decorated with Corinthian columns that seem out of place in this conventional museum, which has exhibits of the city's past history as well as art exhibits. The museum is named after the author Ferenc Móra, who was its director between the two world wars. Open Tues.-Sun. from 10am-6pm.

After visiting the museum you can continue on to the public park in nearby Széchenyi tér. In the square are many statues and also the City Hall, rebuilt in late-Baroque style after the great flood. From here, if you are hungry, you can continue on to the nearby restaurants. We recommend *Debrecen* (No. 13 in the square) and *Szeged* (No. 9 in the square).

The impressive **Synagogue** (Szinagóga) is considered the most beautiful in the country. It was erected on Hajnóczy utca, west of Széchenyi tér, between 1900-1903. Its dome is 48 meters high, and inside it is filled with beautiful objects, the remnants of the wealth and power of the community which was destroyed in the Second World War.

SZEGED

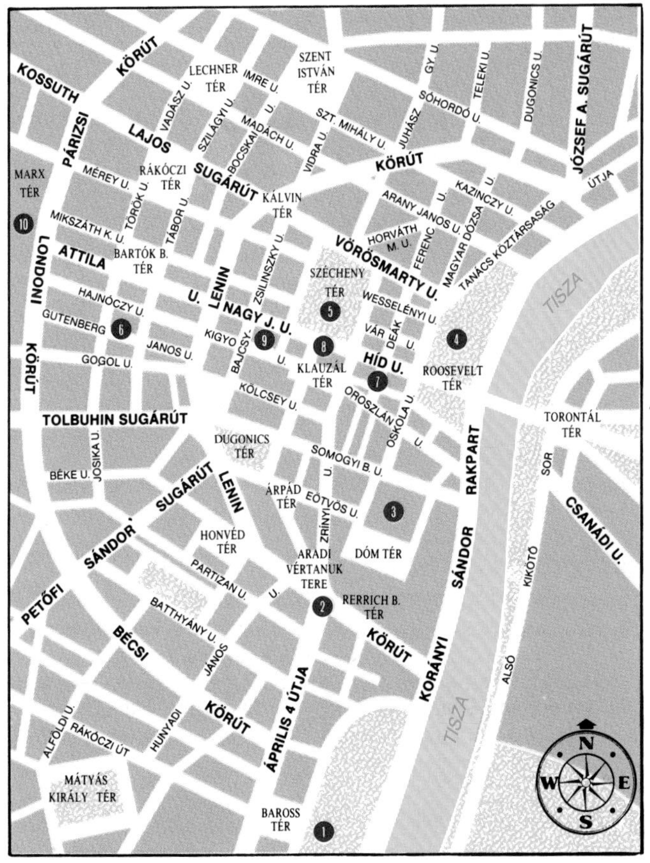

Index

1. Railway station
2. Heroes' Gate
3. Votive Church
4. The municipal museun
5. Public park
6. Synagogue
7. IBUSZ
8. Szeged Tourist
9. Express
10. Bus station

Special events
The Szeged Festival, which begins in mid-July, brings to the city a series of plays and concerts which are held mostly in the open in Dóm tér.

From Szeged onward

Busses leave every weekday for Subotica, Dubrovnik, and Sarajevo in Yugoslavia. Those wanting to continue eastward to the spa town of Gyula (see chapter "Medicinal Baths in Hungary"), 114 kms west of the city on road 47, can also get there by train or bus to Békéscsaba, where you transfer to another bus or train.

Those continuing on to Debrecen, in the northeast part of the country, or to Romania, should travel via Kecskemét and Szolnok.

From Szolnok to Debrecen

Szolnok, 100 kms east of Budapest on road E15, is the crossroads and the railroad junction which serves as a gateway to the plains across the Tisza. It has about 80,000 inhabitants and lies at the confluence of the Tisza and Zagyva Rivers.

Szolnok does not hold any special attraction for tourists, but those spending several hours here waiting for train or bus connections can visit the Franciscan Church (Ferencés Templom), built (1724) in the Baroque style (8 Koltói Anna utca). Then, continue east along the bank of the Tisza to the Tabán district. Here, traditional wooden peasant homes have been preserved, giving some idea of the way of life in the city in previous centuries

For accommodation in Szolnok, make use of the services of the local tourist bureau, *Tiszatour* (32 Ságvári Endre körút, tel. 11-384).

Route E60 continues east for another 84 kms to Püspökladány, before heads for the Romanian border (63 kms from the junction). Those going to Debrecen should continue on road 4 (E573) via the spa town of **Hajdúszoboszló**. The name of the town indicates the origin of some of the region's inhabitants — descendants of the Slavic tribes who revolted against the Turks (hajdú) and fled to this area in order to take cover in the swamps from the oppressive Ottoman regime. In addition to the medicinal spas, which can count on about one million (!) visitors every year, the city contains the remains of walls and a fortress from the 15th century. From here, it is only 25 kms to Debrecen.

Debrecen

Debrecen, the third largest city in Hungary, developed from a tribal center, and has been settled ever since the Stone Age. It first gained prominence as a market town and an economic center in the 14th century, when the Reformation reached the area. At the beginning of the 16th century the city became a Protestant center, and Catholic religious activity was even proscribed here (1552). The Calvinist sect in particular predominated. A Calvinist college was built and is still considered to be one of the best schools in Hungary. There is also a great church, which is the largest non-Catholic church in the country. Today, the city is a Protestant center and an industrial center for farm machinery and food processing. It has about 200,000 inhabitants.

Kálvin tér, where the great church is located, is the center of the old city. Spread out around it, within a short walking distance, you can find most of the tourist attractions in the city, which allows for a comfortable and all-inclusive visit within a few hours.

How to get there

From Budapest, it is easy to reach Debrecen by train from the western railway station. More then ten trains make this 220 km trip daily. It takes 2.5 hours on the express train and about 3.5 hours on the slower local trains. The railway station is located opposite Petőfi tér, from where you can walk to the center on Vörös Hadsereg Street.

There is a very good bus connection to Debrecen from Budapest, as well as from all the eastern sections of the country. From the bus station at Külsővásár tér, walk along Széchenyi utca to the center of town.

Tourist services

Hajdú Tourist is at 20 Vörös Hadsereg utja (tel. 10-820). *IBUSZ* agency is located at No. 11 on that same street (tel. 15-555). *Express* finds lower priced rooms, and it is also located on the same street at No. 77 (tel. 18-332),

The Post Office is located on Hatvan utca, next to the Kálvin tér.

Food and lodging

Aranybika (11-15 Vörös Hadsereg utja, tel. 16-777) is the best and most expensive hotel in the city (three stars). It has tennis courts and a swimming pool.

The *Főnix* (17 Barna utca, tel. 13-355) and *Debrecen* (9 Petőfi tér,

NORTHEASTERN HUNGARY

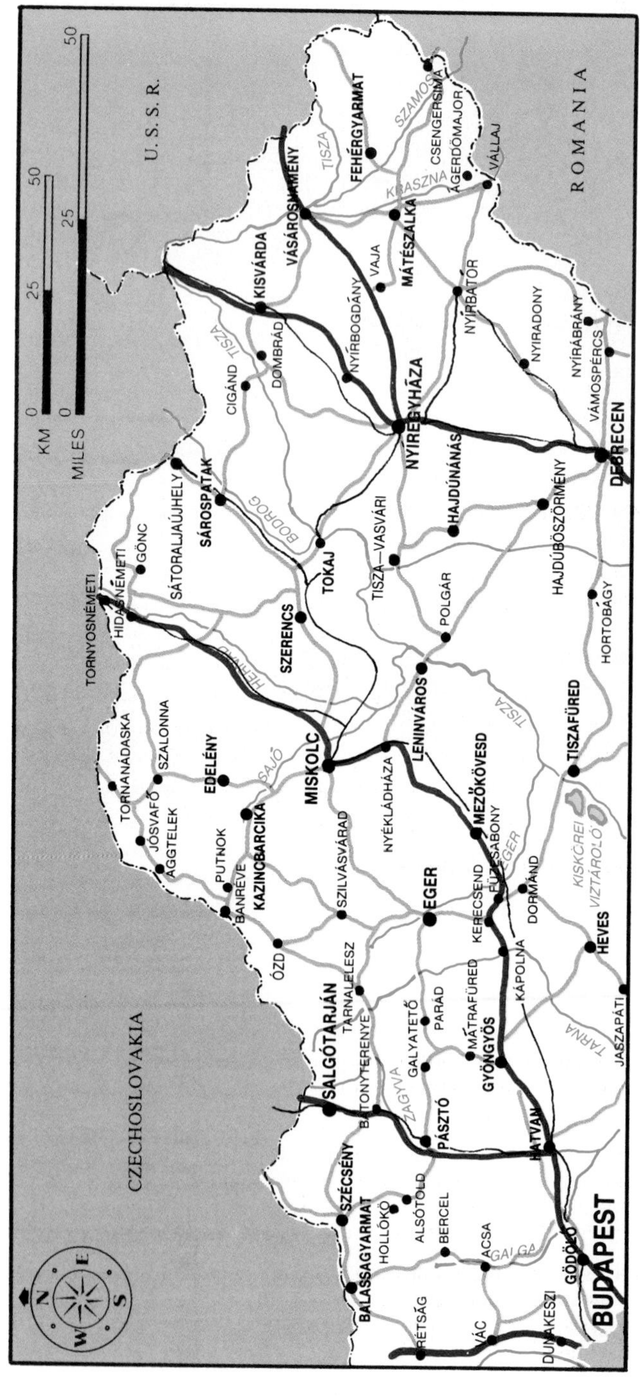

Debrecen — The Calvinist Church

tel. 16-550) are two modest but popular hotels (one-star) located between the train station and the center of town.

In the Nagyerdő Park there are more hotels, including the dependable *Thermál* (9 Nagyerdei körút, tel. 11-888). Some campsites are located outside the city, including the Lake Vekeri Campsite (Vekeri-tó), south of the city, which can be reached via road 47 or by bus 26 from the central bus station in the city.

The best restaurants are along Vörös Hadsereg Street. They include the restaurant of the *Aranybika* at No. 11, the *Gambrinus* at No. 28 (an excellent self-service restaurant and quite cheap), and *Hungária* at No. 53. The many restaurants in the large park, offer cheerful atmosphere and more reasonable prices. Such a restaurant is *Ujvigadó* (tel. 15-085), which is popular among local residents.

What to see

The wide Vörös Hadsereg utja leads north from Petőfi Square to Kálvin tér. House No. 54 on this street, is embellished with lovely capolas. Another attractive building is the old City Hall, built in Art Nouveau style in 1912, which is used today as an office building.

Kálvin tér is dominated by the **Great Church** (Nagy Templom), which faces you as you reach the square. The church was built in the 19th century in neo-Classical style, on the foundations of an ancient church from the 12th century. It can accommodate 5,000 worshippers. The church served as the seat of parliament in 1849, when Hungary proclaimed its separation from the Hapsburg Empire.

The bell in the tower to the left of the church (Rákóczi-Harang) is the largest bell in Hungary. According to tradition, it was cast at the beginning of the 17th century by order of King Rákóczi from a mold weighing five tons.

Behind the Great Church stands the **Calvinist College** (Reformatus Kollégium), built in neo-Classical style in 1803. It replaced the institution which was first erected in the city in 1538, at the height of the religious wave which spread over the country during the Reformation period. Its historical importance, with the huge library of 500,000 volumes, is greater than its architectural significance.

In the **Déri Múzeum** (1 Déri tér), located in a handsome neo-Classical building, there is an exhibit of ancient and new artifacts from the Asian Steppes and a rich anthropological exhibit of daily life in the villages of the Puszta. There is also a modest but interesting exhibit of porcelain from the Far East. Visitors must put on cloth overshoes in order to protect the sensitive wooden floor. (Open during the tourist season Tues.-Sun. from 10am-4pm; during the rest of the year from 10am-4pm.)

While in Debrecen, the large **Municipal Park** (Nagyerdö) offers the visitor thermal baths, botanical gardens and a zoo.

The **Gypsy Market** (Cigány Piac) takes place on Saturdays and Wednesdays in a large field next to the cigarette factory (Dohany Gyár) (Bus No. 30 from the train station). You can find here anything from rusty junk to broken electrical appliances to used clothing. You might even find real bargains and antiques. Beware of pickpockets.

The fruit and vegetable market east of the Great Church is open from the early hours of the morning until 2pm. On weekdays it is interesting and colorful.

The many-hued Carnival of the Flowers on August 20 is a traditional parade of flowers, which ends with a celebration in the stadium and wonderful fireworks from the square beside the Great Church.

Hortobágy National Park (Hortobágy Puszta)

The Hortbágy National Park is located west of Debrecen. The main village in it, Hortobágy, is 26 kms from the city. It can be reached by car on road 33. Those using public transportation can come on the slow local trains from Debrecen or from Tiszafüred, on the other side of the park.

In the park, an effort has been made to preserve the appearance of the prairies and the villages as they were in the past. Attempts have also been made to preserve the many types of fauna which were found in large numbers in the region, such as deer, sheep, boars, and various birds. A famous natural phenomenon in the park is the Fata Morgana (*délibáb* in Hungarian). It occurs mostly to the east of the village of Cserpes and south of the road between Hortobágy and Nagyhegyes. Hikers and visitors, who were lucky have sworn that they have seen thick forests and even small cities on the flat horizon. There is an attractive **Shepherds' Museum** (Pásztormúzeum), open April-September Tues.-Sun. from 9am-12noon and 1pm-6pm.

There are also several modest hotels in the park, such as the *Hortobagy* (tel. 69-071) and *Hortobágy Inn* (Hortobágy Nagy Csárda Fogadó, tel. 69-139) which operate during the tourist season, along with the campsite called *Puszta* (tel. 69-039). The tourist bureau in the Shepherds' Museum will be happy to supply up-to-date information about accommodations.

East from Debrecen

Travellers who want to continue on from Debrecen to the romantic Gypsy villages of popular lore will have trouble finding them. The poor roads and lack of tourist services in this most isolated part of the country make such a visit a bit complicated. But, folklore researchers or lovers of isolated spots will find a trip to this area well worth their time. It can be reached by bus or by hitch-hiking.

For those continuing on to eastern Europe, note that Debrecen is close to the Romanian border, but there are no bus connections.

Winter in the village

The only possibility to cross over into Romania is on the slow train to Valea lui Mihai. Transportation to Moscow and other Russian cities, like the border cities of Cop and Mukacevo, is better.

Northern Hungary

Northern Hungary, the region which stretches from the Czechoslovakian border and the Great Plain to Budapest differs from the other parts of the country, which are mostly flat. This is a region of minor mountain ranges, including the highest mountain in the country — Mt. Kékestető, 1,015 meters high. In spring and summer, the area is covered with green forests, affording possibilities for hikes and vacationers. During the winter, the area is covered with snow.

A trip to the north of the country is also a trip to tranquil farm villages, ancient cities, towns with wonderful wine cellars and stalactite and stalagmite caves, like the one at Aggtelek, which is one of the most outstanding natural wonders in the country.

From Budapest to Eger

Road E71 goes east from Budapest to Eger, with unchanging scenery as it passes among the vineyards which spread from the road as far as the eye can see. It is more interesting to leave this road at the city of Gyöngyös for a visit to the Mátra Mountain Range.

Gyöngyös, with 40,000 inhabitants, is a city with modern residential housing. In the center of the city is a square (Fő tér) which still retains the pleasant 18th century Baroque atmosphere that existed when the city was a central market place for the villages in the area. The large church in the square is **Bertalan Church**, (Szt. Bertalan Templom), built in the 14th century in the Gothic style and renovated with Baroque additions in the 18th century. The **Mátra Múzeum** (40 Kossuth L. utca; open Tues.-Sun. from 9am-5pm), is located east of the central square and has an impressive collection of butterflies, and some exhibits of flora and fauna from these mountains. Additional exhibits describe the wine-growing tradition in the region, typical handicrafts, etc.

Road 24 goes north from Gyöngyös to the Mátra Range. It passes the hilly resort of **Mátrafüred**, which can also be reached by the picturesque train, *Mátravasút*, which leaves from Dimitrov Park in Gyöngyös. Mátrafüred boasts a modern hotel and a campsite where you can stay overnight on your way to Mt. Kékestető, the highest point in all of Hungary.

Mátraháza, located at the beginning of the ascent to the summit of the mountain, at a height of over 700 meters, offers possibilities for lodging and hiking trails. From here, you can go, on foot or by bus, to the summit of **Mt. Kékestető**. At the top, there is a communications tower, nine stories high, and an elevator to the observation balcony which is at 36 meters high (from 9am-3pm on weekdays and until 4pm on weekends). Ski trails and winter cottages can be found to the west of the tower, with cafes and restaurants alongside, some of which rent out inexpensive rooms on the top floor.

Continuing on road 24 toward Eger, it is worth a visit to see the authentic village house (Palóc Ház) in the village of **Parád**, where the atmosphere of the farmers' daily life remains much the same as it has been for hundreds of years. A family that lives in the house behind the site opens it for visitors at all hours of the day.

In nearby **Parádfürdő** there are medicinal baths, and a **Chariot Museum** (Kocsimúzeum), not particularly rich in artifacts, but it is the only one of its kind in the entire country (open Tues.-Sun. from 10am-5pm).

The road continues on to **Recsk**. Here, there was a forced labor camp for people considered to be "enemies of the regime" during the black Stalinist period after the Second World War.

Before reaching Eger, it is worth pausing at the village of **Sirok** near the outskirts. There you will find the ruins of an ancient fortress from the 13th century on the hill overlooking the town, alongside the road. A good "excuse" to take a hike and see the view towards the Bükk Mountains and the Czechosovakian border.

Eger

At the beginning of the 11th century, following the Magyar conquest and the settlement of the Eger Valley, King Stephen established the bishopric in the city. After the city was burnt down and its inhabitants killed by the Mongol invaders in the second half of the 13th century, there was a great renovation effort in the city which lasted until the Turkish siege (1552). The Turks were repulsed and the city remained independent for the next forty years. Only in 1596 did the Turks succeed in conquering the city, which they occupied for the next hundred years.

The golden age of the city was from the middle of the 18th century onward, when it was an important economic center. The accelerated construction in the Baroque style gave the city its present appearance.

The city again suffered from the ravages of war in the middle of the 19th century, when it served as one of the focal points of the revolt, led by Rákóczi, against the Hapsburgs.

Today, about 65,000 people live here, as well as thousands of students who come to study at the universities in the city.

The fortress of Eger overlooks Dobó István tér in the center of town. The main attraction for tourists is the old city, between the fortress and the cathedral. The municipal park (Népkert) in the south (between the railroad station and the center of town) has gardens, a river (Eger patak), and hot springs, in use ever since the Turkish conquest.

How to get there

From Budapest it is possible to get here by bus from the Népstadion Station or by train from the eastern (Keleti) station. The trip takes over two hours. The train station in Eger is located south of the city center. The bus station, from which busses leave for Gyöngyös and Miskolc, is located behind the large cathedral here.

Tourist services

The local *Eger Tourist* (9 Bajcsy-Zsilinsky utca, tel. 11-724) helps with information and advice about touring the city. Other agencies, such as *IBUSZ* (Bajcsy-Zsilinszky tömb Belso, tel. 12-526), *Cooptourist* (3 Dobó tér, tel. 11-998), and *Express* (28 Széchenyi utca, tel. 10-757) are only willing to help people in need of accommodation in the city.

Food and lodging

The *Eger* hotel at the northwest corner of the large park is the best in town, and the quality of its rooms varies with the price (1-3 Szalloda utca, tel. 63-2230). The *Park* at the other end of the building is comfortable.

As to more modest, cheaper hotels, it is best to stay at the *Unicornis* (2 Dr. Hibay K., tel. 12-886) at the foot of the castle, rather than at the less pleasant hostel in Szarvas ter (tel. 11-724) in the center of the old city. These moderately priced rooms cost about the same as private rooms.

The campsite on Rákóczi utca, north of town, can be reached by taxi or by bus No. 10 from the railroad station.

The best restaurants in the city are concentrated in the old city between the fortress and the cathedral. They include the *Széchenyi* restaurant (8 Marx utca) and the excellent, centrally located *Belvarosi* (8 Bajcsy-Zsilinszky utca). Eger is famous

EGER

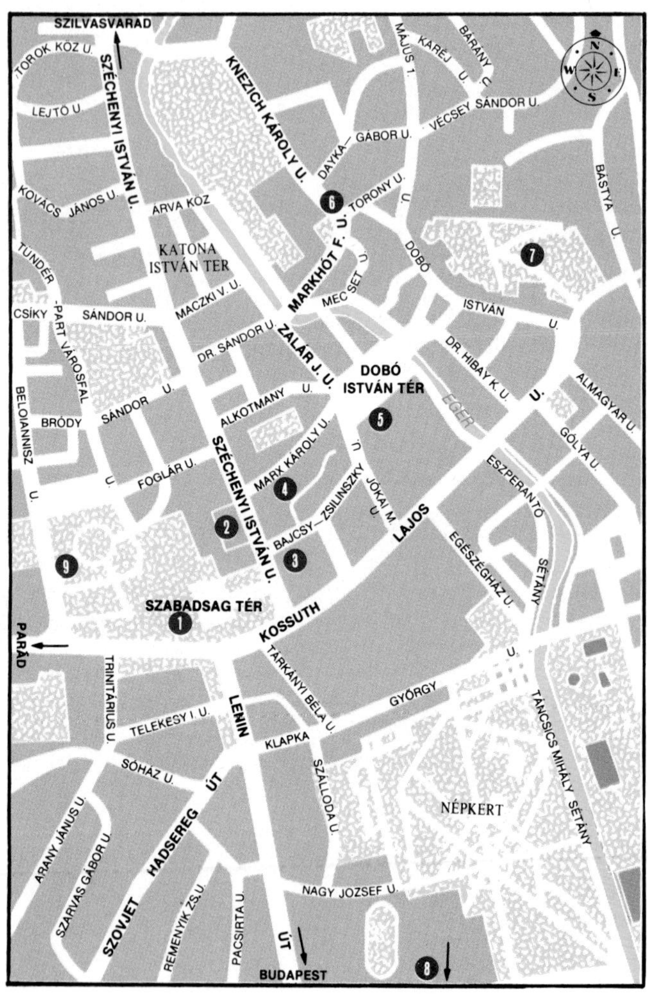

Index

1. The cathedral
2. The bishop's palace
3. Liceum
4. IBUSZ
5. Minorite Church
6. Minaret
7. Eger fortress
8. To the railway station
9. Central bus station

Parád — Town Hall

Picturesque church in the mountainous north

for its wine cellars, around Dósza tér and in Széchenyi Street. Confirmed wine lovers should make a wine excursion to the Szépaszony Valley, west of the city, where there are many vineyards. To reach the valley, take local bus No. 3 from the station in Felszabadulás Square.

What to see

The large **Cathedral** (Bazilika) in Kossuth utca was built 150 years ago by the famous architect József Hild in neo-Classical style. Second largest in the country, the cathedral, impresses more with its grand scale than with its aesthetic sophistication and refinement. The church dome rises to a height of 40 meters, and the Corinthian columns on the facade are 17 meters high. Brief organ concerts are performed during the day, especially for the benefit of large organized touring groups.

The **Bishop's Palace** (Erseky palota), next to the cathedral on the north, was built in the shape of a horseshoe in the 18th century. Facing this religious complex is the former **Christian Lyceum for Girls** (Liceum), built in the Baroque style in the 18th century and one of the largest and most beautiful buildings in this style in all of Hungary. Today it is used for the Ho Chi Minh Teachers' Training College, and there are frequent concerts in its inner courtyard. The **Planetarium** here is open to visitors between the end of May and the end of July, Tues.-Sun. from 9:30am-1pm.

Bajcsy-Szilinszky utca leads from the Catholic school to Dobó Istvan tér in the center of the city, where we find the beautiful **Minorite Church** (Minorita), built in the middle of the 18th century in the Baroque style. Next to it is a monastery of the same name. Notice the sculptures in the square, especially the monument commemorating the Turkish siege.

From the square take a short walk north, in Gerl and Mecset Street, past the open market on the opposite side of the bridge, to the **Minaret**. This is a Turkish prayer tower, built at the beginning of the 17th century, next to a mosque which was destroyed many years ago.

Dobó utca brings us to Dózsa tér, and to **Eger Castle** (vár). It was built in the second half of the 13th century, and won a place of honor in Hungarian history in 1552, when the Turks attacked the city in large numbers. The Hungarians garrisoned themselves in the castle under the command of Dobó István. With the help of the women of the city, they succeeded where many others had failed. They repulsed the attack and withstood the long siege which followed. The encouraging news spread over the entire Christian continent, and many ballads and religious songs were composed and sung by all to honor the heroes of Eger.

In 1596 the fortress was conquered by the Turks, following an attack which lasted only a few days. To this day, the Hungarians blame the multi-national force, which was responsible for the defense of the castle. Later, after the Turks retreated, most of the castle fortifications were destroyed by order of the Hapsburg King Leopold, to prevent supporters of Rákószi from capturing it and thereby controlling the city.

Today, the fortress houses a museum, located in the restored bishop's palace. It contains interesting collections, including Turkish works of art and ancient weapons (open Tues.-Sun. from 9am-5pm). Also in the fortress are underground halls which were used as living quarters and storage rooms and also the Heroes' Hall (Hősök Terme) which commemorates the soldiers and their commander Dobó István. Most rewarding of all is the walk along the walls, from which you can view the city center.

End your tour at the **Municipal Park** (Népkert), for a rest in one of the restaurants or coffee-houses. You can bathe in the crowded pool or in the thermal baths on the east side of the stream which crosses the park.

From Eger to Miskolc

Road No. 3 (E71) is the better road from Eger to Miskolc, but the route is not very interesting. Unquestionably, it is better to go north from Eger on the hilly road which crosses the Bükk Mountains and reach Miskolc from the west. This is one of the most beautiful routes in the country, offering the tourist a wealth of scenic views and mountain villages.

Bükki National Park

The Bükki National Park (Bükki Nemzeti Park), whose name comes from the many beech trees (*Bükk*) in the area, reaches a height of 960 meters, but most of its peaks are around 800 meters high. In this range, which was made into a national park, there are scattered cliffs, breath-taking rock formations, and innumerable cretaceous caves, formed in the limestone rock of which the range is composed.

There are several walking trails in the area, and those who are interested can get a map of the mountain trails from the tourist bureaus in Eger.

For a comprehensive tour of the park, go north from Eger on road No. 25, and after passing the village of **Szarvaskő**, 12 kms from Eger (where you can see the ruins of an ancient

Dobó Square in Eger

Eger — View from the castle

Miskolc Castle

Gypsy women along the way

castle), turn right to **Bélapátfalva**. Here, there is a well-preserved Romanesque church from the beginning of the 13th century.

The **Szilvásvárad Nature Preserve** is one of the most beautiful nature sites in the country. It is worth stopping and going on foot to the green **Szalajka Valley**, with its rivulets and small water falls. Hiking enthusiasts can visit the **Istállóskő caves**, which is about a 40 minute walk.

Continue on the winding road to **Omassa**. This is the starting point for a hike of several hours to the summit of Mt. Balvány, at a height of 956 meters. The road continues on to Lillafüred, on the outskirts of Miskolc.

The best way to tour the Bükk Mountains is in a private car. Those using public transportation should come by bus, which leaves several times daily from Eger to Miskolc. The trip takes less than two hours via the Bükk Mountains, and it is possible to get off the bus, visit some sites, and wait for the next bus. So, while in Eger, get a bus schedule for this route. A number of campsites and hostels are spread throughout the park, for those wanting to stay overnight or longer in the great outdoors.

Miskolc

Miskolc, the second largest city in Hungary, has 215,000 inhabitants. Except for its castle, the city is not an interesting tourist attraction, and despite its size, there is not much reason to visit it. This industrial city with its residential housing projects began its development in the 15th century. It served for a short time as the headquarters of the revolutionary General Rákóczi, at the beginning of the 18th century.

The local tourist bureau (*Borsod Tourist*) is in the center of the city (35 Széchenyi utca, tel. 88-036). *IBUSZ* is also on this same street (No. 1, tel. 18-291), as is *Express* (No. 56, tel. 17-008).

Tourists coming for a short stay can start their tour at the **Greek-Orthodox Church** (Görög Keleti Templom), next to Deák tér. It was built in 1785 by the descendants of Greeks who had come as refugees from the Turks in the 16th century. The Greek settlers brought with them a holy crucifix from Mt. Athos, which was placed in the church and is still kept there. The icon of the Black Virgin of Kazan, one of the holy figures of Greek-Orthodox Christianity, was presented to the church by Czarina Catherine II of Russia.

From the church, walk up Kossuth Lajos utca to the center of the city and to the museum devoted to the history of the city and the nearby Bükk Mountains — **Herman Otto Muzeum** (1 Papszer utca, open Tues.-Fri. from 10am-6pm.)

Queen's Castle (Diósgyor Vár) is in the western suburb, on the way to Lillafüred. This is the most impressive site in the city. It was built as a fortress with four square crenellated towers. Construction began in the middle of the 13th century and lasted for 80 years. King Louis I of the Anjou Dynasty often visited the castle. Later, it was put at the disposal of the Hungarian queens, and from them, it acquired its name. You can enjoy the view from the fortifications and can visit the fortress' museum, Vár Múzeum (24 Vár utca), open April-November Tues.-Sun. from 10am-5pm.

Several kms west of the royal castle is **Lillafüred**, a kind of resort and tourist site which developed around the *Palace* Hotel during the 1930's and 1940's. It has artificial waterfalls and electrically illumnated stalactite and stalagmite caves, which you can forego if you intend to see the Aggtelek Cave.

On from Miskolc

The rural, out-of-the-way region between Miskolc and the Czechoslovakian border invites tourists to improvise, to leave plans flexible rather than choosing a route in advance. This is especially appropriate if you have your own car. You can move freely between the villages, stopping as you like — to see ancient church ruins swallowed up by natural forests, or, in the center of some small village, to notice the farm wives in colorful kerchiefs going about their business. The direction and eventual destination of the trip is the cave at **Aggtelek**, on the Czech border, but take time to wander in the area, on your way to and from the cave.

Aggtelek Cave

The Baradla Cave at Aggtelek is one of the most beautiful and famous in Europe. It is 22kms long. The village of Aggtelek is about 50 kms northwest of Miskolc, and you can reach the cave in a private car or by bus.Some tourist agencies in Budapest and Miskolc make one-day organized trips to the cave.

This large cave, which extends into Czechoslovakia, has several entrances. The main ones are at **Aggtelek** and **Jósvafő**. Most visitors enter from Aggtelek and take a tour of an hour or more in the magic world inside the cave (it is open all year round). The action of the water on the limestone, over a period of millions of years, has created a fantastic landscape of stalactites and stalagmites, which appear to have come straight out of a fairy tale for children. The guides on the tours speak only Hungarian. The cave museum is less interesting than the visit to the cave itself.

The cave is the Number One nature site in the country. Tourists wishing to sleep in the vicinity, can use the services of the travelers' hostel in the village (tel. 6). Near the entrance to the cave is a campsite, which is open to the public during the tourist season.

The Tokaj region

A most pleasant day-long trip can be taken in the Tokay wine region (Tokaj-Hegyalja), including its center, the town of Tokaj, rightly considered to be one of the loveliest towns in the country. The wine region extends across the southern slopes of the Zemplén Mountain Range, which are protected from the cold northeasterly winds while they absorb the sunlight. The location, the volcanic soil, and the long, dry autumn are what make these Tokay wines unique and world famous.

The secret of wine production was already known to local inhabitants in the 4th century BC, and perhaps even earlier. In the 13th century, Hungarian kings brought over Italian and French settlers who were experts in growing grapes and producing wine. In the Middle Ages, word got around the continent, and Polish, German, Russian and other merchants began to come to the wine cellars in the region. Among the aficionados of the local vintage was Pope Pius IV. After tasting the wine during the course of ecclesiastical discussions in 1562, he sighed and said: "Indeed this is a wine fit for the Pope." The philosopher Voltaire argued that Tokay wine possesses qualities which stimulate the brain cells to create words of genius.

About 50 kms east of Miskolc is the town of **Tokaj**, the heart of the region. It can be reached from Miskolc by train, bus, or private car via road 37. The town is located at the confluence of the Tisza and Bodrog Rivers. Settlement began there immediately after the Magyar conquest. Its bucolic landscapes are more impressive than the relics and remains it contains, including the ruins of the **Tokaj Castle**.

In the 15th century the castle was completed, and during the Turkish occupation, it was destroyed. When the local wine became famous throughout the continent, the town became a commercial center and today, about 6,000 people live there.

The **Wine Museum** is on Bethlen Gabor Street. A visit should also be paid to the wine cellar at 13 Kossuth tér, where you can sample various types of this special wine.

In addition to these sites, it is worth wandering through the villages in the region, exploring the hills and vineyards, and buying some of this excellent local product.

Medicinal Baths in Hungary

The Romans who came to Aquincum in the 1st century AD were the first to take advantage of the medicinal baths in Hungary. Ever since, many visitors, both Hungarians and foreigners, have been enjoying these baths. Hot water flows from the depths of the earth, and as it passes through the earth's crust, it absorbs many beneficial minerals.

You can spend as little as a few hours in one of the baths in Budapest, or you can come for a three-week treatment at one of the famous spa towns. The methods of treatment vary, and they include mud baths, hot and cold pools, massages, various exercise methods and equipment, and even drinking the mineral water... All the treatments are done under medical supervision.

The atmosphere in spa towns is rather relaxed, and other than treatment facilities, these towns do not have much to offer. The attitude toward the patient is also not excessively friendly.

Warning: This medical treatment is not recommended for everyone. If you have had any history of illness, you must consult your doctor before coming.

Budapest baths

The baths of Budapest, described in a special section of the chapter on *Budapest*, are also beneficial in the treatment of various ailments. The spring waters which supply the baths in the *Gellért Hotel* contain (among other things) calcium, magnesium, fluorine, carbonic acid, sulphur, and various chlorides. Bathing in these baths is recommended for those suffering from muscle aches and various other disorders.

In the *Csaszar Baths* (35 Frankel Leó út) and the *Lukacs Baths* (No. 29 of the same street) the water is rich in calcium and magnesium, and is even slightly radioactive which makes it particularly suitable for sufferers of muscular aches and chronic bronchitis. The water here flows out from twelve different springs at a temperature of 15-63° Celsius. In the *Rác Baths* (8-10 Hadnagy utca) the temperature of the mineral water reaches 42°Celsius (suitable for sufferers from muscular aches and general fatigue). The *Király Baths* (84 Fő utca) and the *Széchenyi Baths* (in the municipal park in Pest), with their very hot pools, are also good for relaxing muscles and relieving pain.

Spa towns in North Transdanubia

Balf

This town is located next to Lake Fertő, midway between Budapest and Vienna. You can get here by bus from Sopron. The water in the hot springs here contains sulphur, carbonic acid, magnesium carbonate, chlorides, and more. A stay at the spas in the region is suitable mostly for those suffering from digestive and muscular problems. In addition to the baths, it is possible to visit the Catholic church, built in the fourteenth century and renovated in Baroque style.

Those staying here can visit the large estate mansion from the 18th century which has now been converted to a health spa.

Bükfürdő

Thirty kms northeast of Szombathely is the modern spa resort of Bükkfürdő, which developed around the luxurious *Thermál* Hotel (tel. 13-366, telex 37-443). This excellent hotel is the best in the entire area and is quite expensive. The older *Bük Hotel* (tel. 13-363, telex 37-258) is dependable and suited for those on a limited budget. *Szapáry Palace* (Szapáry Kastély), built in the Baroque style in 1696, has been renovated and is now a less pretentious hotel. It is not recommended. You can reach the town by car or by bus from Szombathely.

Here, the thermal water reaches a temperature of 58°Celsius and contains much iron in addition to calcium and magnesium. These baths are especially recommended for arthritic and rheumatic problems.

Sárvár

Sárvár is located 27 kms east of Szombathely. Its 16,000 inhabitants are proud of their rich past, exemplified by the fortress erected in the city on the bank of the Rába River in the 12th century. The 16th century was kind to the city. During that time, it became a center of science and knowledge, as witnessed by the fact that the first book in Hungarian was published here, in 1539. Tourist sites are the castle, renovated in Renaissance style, the gardens of the castle, and the collections kept there.

There are several springs of mineral water here which contain iodine, bromine, sodium, magnesium, and more. This water is good for problems related to joints, nerves, and respiratory ailments. In the prestigious modern *Thermál Hotel Sárvár* (1 Rákóczi utca, tel. 16-088, telex 37-467) a health club has been opened, which also specializes in physiotherapeutic treatments. The hotel also boasts a good dental clinic. Unpretentious *Hotel Mini* (2 Vadkert utca, tel. 228) is not recommended.

Sárvár can be reached on the passenger train from Budapest to Koszeg or by the bus from Sopron, Kőszeg, and Szombathely.

Spa towns in the Balaton area

Balatonfüred

Since the 18th century, Balatonfüred has been attracting many local and foreign visitors, to the northern shore of Lake Balaton, mostly those suffering from cardiovascular ailments. In the past, the waters of the Balatonfüred springs, which contain much carbonic acid, were used as a remedy for digestive trouble, and along with goat-milk water, they were also used to treat respiratory ailments. Since the beginning of this century, the place has become famous as a therapeutic center for those with cardiovascular ailments. The Indian poet Rabindranath Tagore, Nobel Prize Winner for Literature, was among those treated here.

More details about how to reach the town and about accommodation and entertainment can be found in the section devoted to this town in the chapter on Central Transdanubia and Lake Balaton.

Hevíz

Hevíz, located 7 kms northwest of Keszthely, is perhaps the most impressive health center in the country and is one of the largest in central Europe. If in other therapeutic centers we speak of thermal springs which supply the water for the treatment pools, here in Heviz, there is an impressive mineral water lake, extending over twelve acres and reaching a depth of 30 meters. The temperature of the lake water is 30°Celsius, and the flow is so great that the lake water replenishes itself every 28 hours! (the excess water flows via a drainage channel into the Balaton). The lake is of such importance to Hungarians that in 1989 the government decided to close vital mines in the area, which threatened to have a harmful effect on the lake.

In the lake waters, which contain sulphur and carbonic acid, water lilies flower in spring and summer. The water, and especially the mud, is slightly radioactive, and it is excellent for rheumatic ailments, diseases of the joints, and internal infections. The mud is packed and marketed throughout Europe as a natural remedy.

It is easy to get to Hévíz. It can be reached by bus from Budapest, from Vienna and, of course, from nearby Keszthely. *Zalatour* tourist offices. (8 Rákóczi útja, tel. 11-048) and *IBUSZ* (15 Zrinyi M. utca, tel. 35-286) offer many trips around this resort area and help find accommodation at the hotels in the town. Although only 3,500 people live in the town, the tourist agencies offer a wide selection of rooms in private homes, and visitors are directed to these rooms or to the local hotels.

The renowned *Aqua* Hotel (13-15 Kossuth utca, tel. 11-090, telex (35-313) which was built a few years ago is the most modern hotel in town. The nearby *Hévíz* (Nos. 9-11 on the same street, tel. 11-190, telex 35-286) was built in 1976. These two prestigious hotels (4 stars) are open all year and will please even the most finicky of visitors, who will find at their disposal all the services and amenities necessary for their health and comfort.

The *Park* Hotel (26 Petőfi utca, tel. 13-243, telex 35-243) and the *Napsugár*, comfortable and moderately priced, are suitable for conservative tourists with moderate budgets, while the tourist hostel *Gyöngyvirág Turistaszállo* (12 Rákóczi utca, tel. 13-251) open only during the summer season, offers inexpensive sleeping accommodations. In Hévíz, it is possible to find a room to fit almost any budget.

Spa towns in Southern Transdanubia

Harkány

Those coming from Pécs on their way to the Siklós Castle pass through the spa town of Hárkany, 25 kms south of Pécs on road 58, near the Yugoslavian border. The baths were discovered by accident, in the 19th century, by a forest ranger who bathed in the water and was cured of his ailments. The site is popular because of its very hot water (62° Celsius), which contains fluorine and sulphur. The effervescent waters and the mud are especially helpful in treating arthritic and rheumatic ailments and also in gynecological problems.

Tourist services in Harkány include several unpretentious hotels. The best is the *Dràva* (3 Bajcsy-Zs. utca, tel. 80-434). It is preferable to find accomodation outside this flat, quiet town, in pleasant Pécs or at the hotel in the Siklós Castle nearby, and commute to the spa for treatment by car or by local bus. Tourist bureaus in Pécs (see the chapter on *Pécs*) will be happy to provide up-to-date information about anything to do with the spas in the region and arrangements for accommodation.

Spa towns in the Great Plain

Gyula

This quiet spa town, 240 kms southeast of Budapest, is not far from the Romanian border. A therapeutic pool is located in the large park near the castle, which was built in Gothic style at the end of the 14th century, and renovated thirty years ago. The pool water which emerges at a temperature of 70° Celsius contains iodine and bromine, and is beneficial especially for those who suffer from lumbago and spinal ailments.

Tourist attractions include museums, churches from the Baroque period, and sailing on the lake, but none of these are especially inviting. You can reach Gyula by train or bus from Szolnok or from Szeged via Békéscsaba. *Hotel Aranykereszt* (2 Eszperantó tér, tel. 62-144, telex 83-619) is the best in the city and is classed as 3-star. Less expensive rooms can be found in other hotels, pensions, and in private rooms via the *Gyulatourist* office (in *Hotel Aranykereszt*, tel. 61-192).

Hajdúszoboszló

The most moderately priced resort spa seems to be that at Hajdúszoboszló, 20 kms west of Debrecen, on road 4 (E573). The 20,000 inhabitants of the town receive in this spa about one million (!) visitors each year, mostly Hungarians and others from eastern Eurpean countries. Visitors fill the large municipal pools and enjoy the excellent qualities of the water which contains salts, sodium, iron, manganese, lithium, bromine, and which is quite beneficial for ailments of the joints, nervous disorders, and digestive problems. The brown color of the water comes from the iodine and bitumen which it contains in abundance.

Western visitors may be put off by the crowds in public places. We recommend the *Délibáb* Hotel, the best in town (4 József A. utca, tel. 61-788, telex 72-439) where you can enjoy the health facilities it provides. However, arrangements for other accommodations at less pretentious hotels, pensions or rooms in private homes can be made at the local tourist bureau *Hajdútourist* (tel. 60-440), next to the *Délibáb* Hotel. Through this agency, it is also possible to organize trips to the nearby Hortobágy National Park.

Spa towns in Northern Hungary

Parád

The resort town of Parád, about 90 kms east of Budapest on the way to Eger, is located at the foot of the Mátra Hills, on road No. 24, in a pleasant, green area. The waters of the local mineral springs contain sulphur, calcium, magnesium, and more, and they attract many visitors and vacationers, suffering mainly from digestive ailments.

At the Parád spa is the pleasant *Hotel Túra* as well as several pensions and private rooms for rent. You may find it sufficient to bathe for a few hours in the course of a trip to the Mátra mountain range, between Budapest and Eger. In that case, you would not need to sleep over for more than one night, if at all.

Dictionary

In our dictionary we have included commonly used words which the tourist sees or hears often during his visit to Hungary: terms of politeness, words from maps and signs, and other useful words. If you learn to identify these words, it will be easier for you to understand what is happening and to get what you want. Don't underestimate the value of a few polite phrases; they will open doors for you if you manage to pronounce them correctly. For your benefit, we have included a pronuncation key at the end of this dictionary.

Elementary words

yes, ok	*igen, jó*
no	*nem*
please	*tessék*
please	*kérem*
thanks	*köszönöm*
I do not understand	*nem értem*
I am sorry	*sajnálom*
goodbye	*szia*
do not mention it	*szivesen*

General subjects

room	*szoba*
telegram	*távirat*
prohibited	*tilos*
new	*új*
water	*víz*
left	*bal*
right	*jobb*
first	*első*
last	*utolsó*
floor	*emelet*
and...	*és*
main	*fő*
house	*ház*
ticket	*jegy*
small, little	*kis*
large, big	*nagy*
old	*ó, régi*
doctor	*orvos*
help	*segitség*

HUNGARY

Travel

schedule	*menetrend*
motor-cycle	*motorobicikli*
porter	*portás*
airport	*repülötér*
passport	*útlevél*
customs	*vám*
gas-station	*benzinkút*
subway, underground	*főldalatti, métro*
ship	*hajó*
Budapest suburbs train	*HÉV*
car	*kepkocsi*
National Railways	*MÁV*
station	*megállóhely*

Institutions

inn	*csárda*
confectionery	*cukrászda*
café	*eszpresszó*
hospital	*kórház*
grocery store	*közért*
cinema	*mozi*
pharmacy	*patika*
hotel	*szállo*
theater	*szinház*
tobbaconist	*trafik*
restaurant	*véndeglö*
supermarket	*ÁFÉSZ*
gift shop	*ajándék bolt*
shop	*áruház*
restaurant	*étterem*
cinema	*filmszinház*
bath house	*fürdő*
garage	*garázs*
drugstore	*gyógyszertár*
cafe	*kávéház*
gallery	*képtár*
book store	*kőnyvesbolt*

On the map

south	*dél*
cathedral	*dóm*
forest	*erdő*
north	*észak*
spring	*forrás*

hill, mountain	*hegy*
place	*hely*
bridge	*híd*
chapel	*kápolna*
gate	*kapu*
palace	*kastély*
east	*kelet*
lookout	*kilátó*
park	*park*
railway station	*pályaudvar (pu.)*
market	*piac*
platform, quay	*rakpart*
esplanade	*sétány*
row	*sor*
saint	*szent (szt.)*
island	*sziget*
camp	*tábor*
church	*templom*
square	*tér, körtér*
lake	*tó*
block	*tömb*
tower	*torony*
court, yard	*udvar*
avenue	*út (útja)*
street	*utca (u.)*
citadel	*vár*
town	*város*
town center	*városközpont*
boulevard	*körút*
alley	*köz*
well	*kút (-ja)*
grove	*liget*
monument	*műemlék*
embassy	*nagykövetség*
west	*nyugat*
road	*országút*

Signs

open	*nyitva*
box office	*pénztár*
money change	*pénzváltás*
vacant	*szabad*
dangerous	*veszélyes*
look out!	*vigyázat!*
closed	*zárva*
entrance	*bejárat*

men	*férfiak*
occupied	*foglalt*
exit	*kijárat*
slow (driving)	*lassan*
toilets	*mosdó, W.C.*
women	*nők*

Days of the week

Monday	*hétfő*
Tuesday	*kedd*
Wednesday	*szerda*
Thursday	*csütörtök*
Friday	*péntek*
Saturday	*szombat*
Sunday	*vasárnap*

Numbers

0	*nulla*
1	*egy*
2	*kettö*
3	*három*
4	*négy*
5	*öt*
6	*hat*
7	*hét*
8	*nyolc*
9	*kilenc*
10	*tíz*
11	*tizenegy*
12	*tizenkettő*
13	*tizenhárom*
14	*tizennégy*
15	*tizenöt*
16	*tizenhat*
17	*tizenhét*
18	*tizennyolc*
19	*tizekilenc*
20	*húsz*
21	*huszonegy*
22	*huszonkettő*
23	*huszonhárom*
30	*harminc*
31	*harmincegy*
40	*negyven*
50	*ötven*
60	*hatvan*

70	*hetven*
80	*nyolcvan*
90	*kilencven*
100	*száz*
101	*százegy*
150	*százötven*
200	*kettöszáz (kétszáz)*
300	*háromszáz*
400	*négyszáz*
500	*ötszáz*
600	*hatszáz*
700	*hétszáz*
800	*nyolcszáz*
900	*kilencszáz*
1000	*egyezer (ezer)*
2000	*kétezer*

Pronunciation key

In Hungarian, the accent falls on the first syllable and only rarely on any other syllable.

Consonants

ny	*nie*	*like in "new"*
s	*sh*	*like in "ship"*
sz	*s*	*like in "small"*
ty	*tie*	
zs	*j*	*like in "jail"*
dsz	*g*	*like in "George"*
c	*tc*	
cs	*ch*	*like in "Charles"*
gy	*die*	
j	*ie*	
ly	*ye*	

Note:
When the letter "l" comes before "y", it is not pronounced at all.
The combination "dzs" almost always denotes a word of foreign origin.
The letter "h" coming after "c" or "s" does not make a diphtong and is pronounced separately as "h".

HUNGARY

Vowels
long:

á	*aa*	
é	*ee*	
í	*e*	*like in "seen"*
ó	*o*	
ú	*ou*	*like in "house"*
ő	*oe*	
ű	*ue*	

short:

a	*a*	*like in "last"*
e	*e*	*like in "length"*
i	*e*	*like in "little"*
o	*o*	*like in "old"*
u	*oo*	*like in "wood"*
ö	*ö*	
ü	*ü*	

INDEX

Budapest

INDEX

NOTES

NOTES

NOTES

NOTES

NOTES

NOTES

QUESTIONNAIRE

In our efforts to keep up with the pace and pulse of Hungary, we kindly ask your cooperation in sharing with us any information which you may have as well as your comments. We would greatly appreciate your completing and returning the following questionnaire. Feel free to add additional pages. A complimentary copy of the next edition will be sent to you should any of your suggestions be included.

Our many thanks!

To: Inbal Travel Information (1983) Ltd.
18 Hayetzira Street
Ramat Gan 52521
Israel

Name: ______________________________

Adress: ______________________________

____

Occupation: ______________________________

Date of visit: ______________________________

____

Purpose of trip (vacation, business, etc.): ______________

____

____

Comments/Information: ______________________________

____

____

____

____

____

____

____

____

____

____

____

____

1/91

INBAL Travel Information Ltd.
P.O.B. 39090 Tel Aviv
ISRAEL 61390